# Chasing the Same Signals

## How Black-Box Trading Influences Stock Markets from Wall Street to Shanghai

# Chasing the Same Signals

## How Black-Box Trading Influences Stock Markets from Wall Street to Shanghai

Brian R. Brown

**WILEY**

John Wiley & Sons (Asia) Pte. Ltd.

Published in 2010 by John Wiley & Sons (Asia) Pte. Ltd.,
2 Clementi Loop, #02-01, Singapore 129809

*Other Wiley Editorial Offices*

John Wiley & Sons, Inc., 111 River Street, Hoboken, NJ 07030, USA
John Wiley & Sons, Ltd., The Atrium, Southern Gate, Chichester, P019 8SQ, UK
John Wiley & Sons (Canada), Ltd., 5353 Dundas Street West, Suite 400, Toronto, Ontario M9B 6HB, Canada
JohnWiley & Sons Australia Ltd., 42 McDougall Street, Milton, Queensland 4064, Australia
Wiley-VCH, Boschstrasse 12, D-69469 Weinheim, Germany

*Library of Congress Cataloging-in-Publication Data*

ISBN-13: 978-0-470-82488-7

Typeset in 10.5/13pt Palatino by Laserwords Private Limited, Chennai, India.
Printed in Singapore by Toppan Security Printing Pte. Ltd.

10 9 8 7 6 5 4 3 2 1

*To Donna,*
*for everything we share.*

# Contents

# Acknowledgments

A few years ago, I was enjoying dinner with a group of eight colleagues and clients at a Cantonese restaurant at the Lee Garden in Hong Kong. Looking across the table I realized there were not two people of the same nationality, nor were any living in their country of origin. A career on Wall Street, despite all the perceptions, is a platform to enrich one's life experience within a truly global community. I am grateful to those who have provided me these wonderful opportunities, and I acknowledge much of my maturity and contentment has arisen out of the interactions along the way.

A variety of former colleagues and business associates were engaged on the book's concepts. I much appreciate the perspectives and insights of Robert Ferstenberg, Amit Rajpal, Peter Sheridan, Marc Rosenthal, Kurt Baker, E. John Fildes, Robert S. Smith, John Feng, and Tom Coleman; you are all the best at what you do.

During the initial drafts, Paul Leo, whose candid feedback, although sobering, was an instrumental catalyst to improve the breadth of research and adherence to the thesis; much appreciation for your editorial insights and professionalism.

To my friends Tony Behan and Madeleine Behan, at *The Communications Group*, for providing timely advice at the onset of my aspiration to become a writer. The regular breakfast forums were the best discipline throughout this journey.

To Nick Wallwork, Fiona Wong, Cynthia Mak, and the team at *John Wiley & Sons*, for bringing this book to fruition. You're all wonderful ambassadors of a truly first-class firm.

A great variety of friends and acquaintances maintained an interest in hearing about the various stages of my transition as a writer. Thank you to Andrew Work, Charles Poulton, Neil Norman, Greg Basham, Mohammed Apabhai, Jeremy Wong, Godwin Chan and Martin Randall.

Most importantly, I thank my wife, Donna, for tolerating my wandered mind that sporadically drifted throughout the entire authoring process, and so on. I am indeed the luckiest man alive.

And finally, to my parents, Robert and Carole, for their constant support and enthusiasm, from Talbot Street to Nathan Road.

# CHAPTER 1

# The Canary in the Coal Mine

## *How the First Signal of the Financial Crisis Wasn't Noticed*

A year before the financial tsunami of October 2008 materialized and the words "subprime mortgages" became common language ingrained in our evening news, there was a subtle warning in the financial markets that the world's global economies were not in a state of balance. The warning materialized in the first week of August 2007, when global equity markets observed the worst stockmarket panic since Black Monday in October 1987. But nobody noticed.

On the morning of August 6, 2007, investment professionals were baffled with unprecedented stock patterns. Mining sector stocks were up 18 percent but manufacturing stocks were down 14 percent. It was an excessive 30 percent directional skew between sectors, yet the S&P index was unchanged on the day.

The next few days would continue with excessive stock volatility and dispersion patterns. MBI Insurance, a stock that had rarely attracted speculation would finish up 15 percent on August 6, followed by another 7 percent on August 7, and then finish down 22 percent over the subsequent two days. The rally in MBI was nothing more than an aberration as the gains reversed as quickly as they appeared.

Conventional wisdom suggests markets are efficient, random walks—stock prices rise and fall with the fundamentals of the company and preferences of investors. But on August 8, the housing sector would be the best performing in the market with a gain of 22 percent. Certainly, there was a deviation from "fundamental" values amid the emerging worries of a U.S. housing crisis.

Only weeks later would investors begin to have insights on the dispersion patterns. Prominent hedge funds that had never had a negative annual performance began disclosing excessive trading losses,

1

with many notable managers reporting several hundred millions were lost—in a single day.

Hedge funds were haemorrhaging in excess of 30 percent of their assets while the S&P index was unchanged. They were losing on both sides of the ball—their long positions were declining and their short positions were rising. Sectors that were normally correlated were moving in opposite directions.

The market dispersion was the side effect of hedge funds synchronous portfolio "de-leveraging," ignited by a deviation in equity markets from their historical trading patterns. It was the industry's first worldwide panic—by machines.

In the late 1990s, the Securities and Exchange Commission (SEC) introduced market reforms to improve the efficiency of the marketplace to allow for alternative trading systems—this marked the birth of electronic communications networks, as well as a new era of quantitative investment professionals. Over the past decade, computerized (or black-box) trading has become a mainstream investment strategy, employed by hundreds of hedge funds.

Black-box firms use mathematical formulas to buy and sell stocks. The industry attracts the likes of mathematicians, astrophysicists, and robotic scientists. They describe their investment strategy as a marriage of economics and science.

Their proliferation has come on the back of success. Black-box firms have been among the best performing funds over the past decade, the marquee firms have generated double-digit performance with few if any months of negative returns. Their risk-to-reward performance has been among the best in the industry.

Through their coming of age, these obscure mathematicians have joined the ranks of traditional buy-and-hold investors in their influence of market valuations. A rally into the market close is just as likely the byproduct of a technical signal as an earnings revision.

It has been speculated that black-box traders represent more than a third of all market volume in the U.S. markets and other major international markets, such as the London Stock Exchange (LSE), German Deutsch Boerse and Tokyo Stock Exchange (TSE), albeit their contributions to the daily markets movements go largely unnoticed. CNBC rarely comments on the sentiments of computerized traders.

Our conventional understanding of the stock market is a barometer for the economy. Stock prices reflect the prevailing sentiment on the health of the economy and the educated views of the most astute investment professionals. But what has become of the buy-and-hold investor when holding periods have slipped from years to months to days (or less)?

Although their success has largely been achieved behind the scenes, the postmortem of the August 2007 crisis brought black-box firms into the headlines. Skeptics suggested the demise of quantitative trading was a matter of time given that stock prices are a random walk.

But many black-box firms have weathered the market turbulence and continued to generate double-digit returns. They were the first hedge funds to experience the economic tsunami that would evolve into a widespread global crisis in 2008, when markets drifted from their historical patterns.

Adaptation, after all, has always been their lifeblood. Their investment strategy is a zero-sum game; they do not benefit from prosperous economic climates when the rising tide lifts all boats. Black-box traders compete with one another by *chasing the same signals.*

This is not a story about what signals they chase, but rather a story about how they chase them. It's a story about how an industry of automated investors, with unique risk preferences and investment strategies, have become the most influential liquidity providers from Wall Street to Shanghai.

## THE SIGNAL OF IMBALANCE

On the morning of August 6, 2007, the canary on the trading floor of the world financial markets would stop singing. There was a foul smell in the air, resonating from the world economy, and it had materialized in the form of an early warning detection signal. World stock markets would begin to observe a unique form and unprecedented type of volatility. It was an early indication that the state of the global economy was at an inflection point of imbalance.

Just one hour into the morning session on August 6, traders in the S&P 500 would begin to observe some very unusual price patterns on their trading screens. The machinery sector was up 10 percent while the metals sector was down 9.5 percent. There was a net difference of 20 percent between the sectors, yet there was little news or earnings information to support such a direction skew between sectors.

Despite the excessive volatility across sectors, the S&P index was unchanged on the day at 0.2 percent from the previous day's close. Gains in one sector were being offset by losses in another.

Looking closer at the S&P 500 components was even further confusing—there were more than 50 stocks trading up 10 percent and 50 stocks down more than 10 percent. Yet the index as a whole was relatively unchanged.

Traders were confused. What was going on in the market? Who would be aggressively buying a portion of the index and aggressively selling the other side?

Traders would find no clues when speaking to their institutional clients. Mutual fund managers were equally as baffled by the confusing price charts. August was normally a quiet month, and there had been no release of major economic news and none was expected on the immediate horizon.

The unusual trading patterns of excessive dispersion would continue for the next several days. Many stocks were batted around for the entire week, taking huge gains one day and then snapping back to their previous level the next.

The unusual market volatility would spread from U.S. markets to Europe to Japan. These were unprecedented times in global equity markets, it was the greatest level of "dispersion" observed in history.

Dispersion, the difference between its best and worst performers, has historically been within a range of a few percentage points across S&P 500 stocks within a given day. The index's best performer might be up 5 percent and the worst down 4 percent. On August 6, 2007, the dispersion of S&P 500 constituents was all over the map (see figure 1.1). The best and worst stocks were 32 percent apart. This had never happened before.

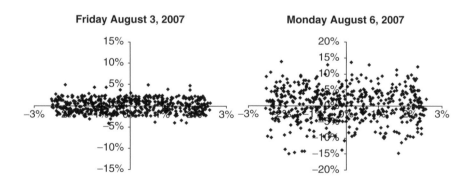

**FIGURE 1.1**  S&P index dispersion
Note: Scatter plot of that day's price movement against the previous day's price movement

Insights into the market volatility would begin to surface in the first weeks of September when several notable hedge funds began to communicate to their investors that they had taken excessive losses during the month of August. The first week of August, several funds reported declines in excess of 30 percent of their holdings. A couple of the most prominent hedge funds reported to have suffered losses of a few hundred million dollars in a single day.

These were not just a random collection of hedge funds that had an off month. These were a collection of the most prominent hedge funds, known as "quant" funds because they use complex mathematical models to invest in markets around the globe. Despite having produced some of the most consistent returns for the past decade, a similar story was being reported across the spectrum of managers. Articles appearing in a variety of sources highlighted a common tail of woes across several "star" hedge fund managers:

> Star managers racked up hefty mark-to-market losses within the first 10 days of August. **Renaissance Technologies'** institutional equities fund had lost −8.7 percent as of August 9; **Highbridge** statistical opportunities fund suffered −18 percent monthly decline; **Tykhe Capital's** statistical arbitrage and quantitative long/short masters funds ranged from −17 percent to −31 percent as of August 9; **Goldman Sachs Asset Management** global equities opportunities fund bled over −30 percent as of August 10; **D.E. Shaw's** composite fund was down −15 percent as of August 10; **Applied Quantitative Research's** flagship fund plummeted −13 percent between Aug 7 and Aug 9; **Morgan Stanley's Proprietary Trading** reported losses in their quantitative strategies of approximately $480 million, most of which occurred in a single day.[1]

These "star" managers had one thing in common: their investment strategy was faltering for no apparent reason. Historical patterns were breaking down. Similar stocks that in historical periods were highly correlated were now moving in opposite directions. The value sector, which normally outperformed the growth sector during periods of market dislocation, was now doing the opposite: growth outperformed value.

Hedge funds were suffering losses on both sides of their portfolio. Their long positions were declining and their short positions were rising. Portfolios that had been optimized to minimize variance were observing unpredictable volatility. Hedging long/short positions was intended to reduce the risk of a market correction, but they were experiencing a different kind of chaos event—dispersion. In a matter of days, they would take losses of upward of a third of their assets, when

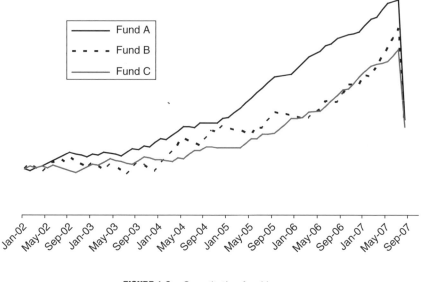

**FIGURE 1.2**   Quantitative fund losses
Note: Fund assets have been normalized from a base value of 1.0

their previous worst monthly declines had been a couple percentage points (see figure 1.2).

The canary had stopped singing because the global markets were at the beginning of a period of great imbalance between the equity markets and credit markets. Financial institutions were just starting to enter a prolonged process of "de-leveraging" in which they would reduce their equity positions to offset losses on subprime mortgage debt.

## THE CROWDED TRADE EFFECT

A postmortem of the August 2007 quantitative funds meltdown would be inconclusive. There is no industry watchdog that could reverse engineer the set of computerized strategies. Understanding the nature of the problem would be further compounded by the secrecy of the "black-box" community, who are known for their privacy and seclusion, preferring the quiet suburbs of Connecticut or Chicago to the bright lights of Wall Street. The evidence from industry analysts and professionals was obvious: it was clear that most of these hedge funds were holding similar positions.

The most likely catalyst is that one or more large quantitative funds were forced into liquidation during the first week of August, possibly because of subprime losses in other areas of the fund, and to increase cash flow (or to raise balance-sheet assets), the fund flattened its quantitative strategies portfolio.[2] August 6, 2007 is likely the industry's first instance of what would become widespread in October 2008: de-leveraging.

A portfolio unwinding its positions wouldn't normally be a problem: unless there were several other funds holding the same positions. When the instigator begins to unwind, its trading would move the market; short positions would rise and long positions would decline. The other funds holding those same holdings would begin to suffer losses as their positions moved against them. As losses worsen, at some threshold, a fund might begin to reduce its own positions, perhaps decreasing its portfolio by 20 percent or more. Their unwinding, however, would both compound losses and start a chain reaction across the universe of funds holding the same portfolios.

This theory assumes that many quantitative funds were holding similar positions, which is known as the "crowded trade" phenomenon. When one firm began to liquidate, the other fund managers who were holding similar positions began to take losses as the positions reversed. This triggered a "run for the exits" phenomenon that moved markets to unprecedented patterns of dispersion.

The crowded trade theory is based on an assumption that black-box fund managers were employing a similar strategy. This may seem far-fetched—Renaissance, D.E. Shaw, Goldman Sachs, Highbridge—these were the marquee firms, presumably the "rocket scientists" of finance; was it a fair assumption to suggest their computer models were all chasing the same signals?

Although there is no hard evidence to decipher the strategies employed across the industry, there is evidence to support the contention that quantitative hedge funds were holding similar positions. One of the underpinnings of quantitative strategies was the empirical significance that value stocks would outperform growth stocks in times of market distress.

In practical terms, investors could profit from adopting a "contrarian" strategy, in which they sell all the winners and buy all the losers. This is the classic mean-reversion strategy, in which quantitative traders sell stocks that have outperformed the market and buy stocks that have underperformed, hedging the two sides based on historical correlations.

The postmortem of the events of August 2007 observed that historical relationships were breaking down across sectors. Technical studies highlighted that the one-month correlation between value and growth stocks had increased by 20-fold in the first week of August. Sectors that normally would have been good candidates for long/short hedging were moving in the opposite direction to their historical patterns. And any strategy trained on hedging based on historical correlations would have been susceptible to losses, regardless of the signals they had been chasing.

What had become painfully obvious in the wake of August 2007 turmoil was just how large and influential the footprint that quant models had attained in the global financial system. How did a handful of mathematicians and physicists grow to have so much influence on the valuations of global markets from Wall Street to Shanghai?

## THE BLACK-BOX PHENOMENON

Quantitative trading had been around for decades, but in the late 1990s the industry underwent a massive transformation owing to newly available electronic trading technology, which lowered the costs of trading and provided access to global equity markets from a single location, whether New York or Des Moines. Correspondingly, quantitative trading blossomed into a new industry of "black-box" strategies.

A "black box" is a quantitative investment strategy in which the decisions are defined by mathematical formulas. Black-box firms design models to predict market movements based on analysis of historical trading patterns. Black-box firms rely on computerized implementation of their models to trigger the buying and selling of assets, so the prerequisite of a black-box model is to be an automated trading algorithm.

Firms that employ a black-box model are often referred to as "quants" because they employ mathematicians, physicists, and computer scientists, rather than the traditional MBAs and fundamental research analysts. They typically engineer their models to target small price movements, rather than search for long-term investment opportunities. Their holding periods might range from weeks to hours to minutes, rather than 12–18 months like a mutual fund.

These firms prosper on their ability to capitalize on "price discrepancies," and most are agnostic to the long-term valuation of the stocks they hold. Their businesses thrive on liquidity and volatility, rather than the economic growth that traditional investors depend on for prosperity.

The language of "black box" originated out of the obscurity of the investment strategy. Investors began vaguely to refer to any strategy as a black box if the investment decisions were contained within formulas and equations. The analogy to the real aviation black box for the most part has been quite fitting—investors aren't really sure what happens on the inside.

The events of August 2007 not only turned the investment community's attention to black-box firms, but also raised awareness of how prominent quantitative trading had become over the past decade. It is not a single type of strategy, nor is it confined to hedge funds. Rather, a diverse variety of investment firms employ quantitative and algorithmic trading strategies.

A formal definition of a "black-box strategy" would be any trading system that relies on an empirical model to govern the timing and quantity of investment decisions. The prerequisite for the black-box description is automation through computerized trading algorithms.

The distinction between black-box strategies is much broader than simply the formulas and equations that govern the timing of their trading. A black-box strategy is distinct not only in the "signals" that trigger its trading decisions but also its investment objective and risk preferences. Even two computers that are monitoring the same market events may transact on the same signals in unique ways, differing by the entry and exit levels, holding period, and hedging methodologies.

*Trend following (or momentum)* is the best-understood form of black-box trading. Mathematical models are designed to forecast the stock price movement. The model is attempting to quantify the inflection points in the market and to profit by trading alongside the initiation of a trend and taking profits when a new price level has been reached.

*Statistical arbitrage (or statarb)* is a more complex form of quantitative trading than directional trend-following strategies. These models attempt to exploit price anomalies in correlated securities. They typically are nondirectional (therefore the term arbitrage) in that they buy one security and sell another, hoping to profit on the difference between the price margins of the directional positions.

The basic understanding of a statarb strategy is best expressed through a simple mean-reversion strategy between correlated securities, such as Coke and Pepsi or GM and Chrysler. The statarb strategy monitors the "margin" between these pairs of correlated securities and takes a position when the margin increases (or decreases) to a statistically significant distance from its historical mean.

*Market-neutral strategies* are a more comprehensive extension of combinations of correlated stocks. This investment strategy's objective is to manage portfolios of hundreds of stocks in equal dollar weight of long positions to short positions. These strategies can also enforce other types of neutral constraints, such as beta-neutral (balanced to the index movements), gamma-neutral (balanced to market volatility) or sector-neutral (dollar balanced per sector).

Market-neutral managers often trade in hundreds of securities to distribute risks across a broad spectrum of sectors and industries. They devise multifactor models using every imaginable type of financial information—balance sheets, risk factors, economic data, and analysts' forecasts—to rank the relative value of stocks.

*Automated market making (AMM)* has been the most recent evolution of black-box trading thanks to advancements in electronic commerce networks (ECNs) and liberalization of equity markets, such as decimalization and regulatory reforms. Automated market makers provide liquidity to investors, similar to the role of a traditional specialist or market maker, by being the intermediary on transactions between buyers and sellers, profiting on the difference between bid-to-offer prices for the risk of holding inventory momentarily.

AMM firms introduced technology to the process, designing algorithms to quote bids and offers to the investment community simultaneously across thousands of securities. These are the most high-frequency trading firms, transacting millions of orders a day and carrying few (or no) positions overnight.

*Algorithmic trading (algos)* strategies are the brokerage industry's contribution to black-box trading. These are automated strategies that manage an order's execution, usually optimized to minimize slippage to an industry benchmark, such as volume weight average price (vwap) or arrival price.

Traditional asset managers leverage these algos to improve the efficiency of their execution desks by automating the execution of small orders and unwinding block trades using financially engineered models. Electronic trading allowed them to streamline their businesses, reduce the tail of stocks transactions, and concentrate on their order flows that demanded liquidity. Within a few years of electronic trading commencing, traditional asset managers were executing as much as 20 percent of their order flows through algos.

The growth of black-box trading is better described as a "phenomenon," the period in history when equity markets became largely dominated by computer-to-computer interactions as hedge funds, institutional investors, brokerage houses, and proprietary trading firms all moved in parallel to leverage electronic trading technology. In less than a decade after the arrival of electronic trading technology, computers would grow to become the most active investors.

## THE EVOLUTION OF QUANTS

The origins of black-box trading are not constrained to one firm or period. The maturity of electronic trading technology was an iterative process, and there has been much resistance to inhibit its growth. Hedge funds, brokerages, and institutional investors each moved at a different pace in adopting technology by exploring areas in which electronic trading could complement their business strategy and revenue growth.

The most eager adopters of electronic trading were the multistrategy hedge funds and commodity trading advisors that had heavily leveraged quantitative research. Renaissance Technologies, D.E. Shaw, Trout Trading Management Co., and The Prediction Company were among the early quantitative hedge funds to pioneer high-frequency trading strategies. They would be among the few examples of hedge funds to market themselves as dedicated "quant" funds.

The largest multistrategy hedge funds have been the pioneers in this space; Citadel, Highbridge Capital, Two Sigma, SAC Capital, and Millennium Partners all are anecdotally thought to be several percentage points of U.S. market volume. Although it's only one facet of their businesses, black-box trading has become a large part of their footprint in the financial markets.

The major brokerage houses were some of the earliest and most aggressive sponsors of technical trading. They had the trading infrastructure to leverage their customer technology within proprietary trading groups. Goldman Sachs' Quantitative Alpha Strategies and Morgan Stanley's Process Driven Trading (PDT) were two of the most successful quantitative trading groups that would grow to rival the top-tier hedge funds in both performance and assets under management.[3]

Market-neutral investing blossomed in line with the maturity of electronic trading technology. Applied Quantitative Research (AQR) Capital, Black Mesa Capital, Numeric Investments, Marshall Wace, which were early entrants in market-neutral investment, grew into multibillion dollar funds. They would also employ the highest leverage in the industry, so they would trade hundreds of millions each day while rebalancing their long/short portfolios.

Electronic trading changed the economics of the quantitative investment strategies because it made markets more accessible to remote participants and it dramatically lowered the costs of trading. What the trading infrastructure did for a firm based in Santa Fe was to make it just as easy to execute on the LSE as on the Australian Stock Exchange. New opportunities were the result.

Correspondingly, the daily gyrations of the stockmarket are now largely influenced by the interactions among computerized investors, each pursuing their unique investment objectives, risk preferences, and trading logic.

## WHAT SIGNALS ARE THEY CHASING?

In finance, the "efficient market hypothesis" has been one of the most widely accepted theories for the better part of three decades. The theory asserts that stock prices reflect all known information and they adjust instantaneously to new information. Since its initial publication by Eugene Fama in the 1960s, many academic studies have reiterated that stock prices do move along a "random walk," and that investors cannot earn excess returns from speculating on news, earnings announcements, or technical indicators.

Despite all the evidence that markets are random, there is a sufficient body of academic research to contradict the theory—that markets observe periods of historical "price anomalies." A price anomaly is an irregularity or deviation from historical norms that recurs in a data series. If investors can find these patterns, they can earn superior returns from exploiting the market inefficiency.

There are many anecdotal views on the existence of price anomalies due to the predictable behavior of investors, caused by overreacting to new information or by suffering from irrational risk aversion. Anomalies are manifested in seasonal effects, post-earnings drift, and events such as price reversals on news announcements. They can be rationalized with economic reasons, such as how investors react to surprise earnings announcements, or they can be rationalized by subtle and illogical causes, such as weather or seasonal effects.

There is a great body of academic research to quantify the existence of price anomalies. Researchers at New York University performed a 25-year study of the S&P 500 index from 1970 through 2005 to assess the "day of the week" effects, and they concluded that Mondays have the lowest expected returns of the week. An investor would have outperformed the market by buying on Wednesdays rather than Mondays.

Academics also suggest that market structure can create inefficiencies from differing tax regulation or the trading mechanisms. Future contract expiry days, for instance, may create imbalances in the market given the number of investors trying to roll their contracts from one month to the next. Many studies have confirmed that the last hour of trading on key monthly expiry dates observes accelerated market volatility.

Quantitative investors, by definition, are advocates of market inefficiency. They hold a belief in the existence of price anomalies and they dedicate elaborate efforts to devise models that quantify market behavior. The field of quantitative finance (also referred to as financial engineering) is a rich and diverse field, attracting all types of scientific disciplines from mathematics, economics, and the physical sciences.

Researchers use many resources to search for price anomalies. There is a seemingly infinite array of empirical metrics for analysts to search for inefficiencies. There are hundreds of empirical metrics on a stock's financial performance: price-to-earnings ratio, price-to-book ratio, debt-to-equity, year-to-date return, earnings growth, dividend yield, and so on. Similarly, macroeconomic information and surveys are released almost every week to update the investment community on unemployment levels, retail spending, inflation, and many other relevant metrics that influence the market's valuation.

Over the past decade, market data vendors such as Thomson Reuters, the Organization for Economic Co-operation and Development (OECD), and MSCI Barra have institutionalized vast arrays of financial metrics that are archived regularly across thousands of public securities. The standard sets of financial data fall into a few broad categories: balance-sheet, market data, risk factors, and macroeconomic data.

*Balance-sheet* metrics are the set of accounting metrics that describe a company's balance-sheet and cash-flow properties: debt-to-equity, earnings per share, expense ratio, and so on.

*Market data* indicators are the technical variables derived from trading data, such as the last trade price, open, high, low, close, and volume.

*Macroeconomic data* are statistics that affect the broad economy, such as unemployment or retail sales.

*Risk factors* are estimates of a stock's sensitivity to relevant industry factors: oil, interest rates, inflation, and so on.

Quantitative investors look at each and every available data series to search for market anomalies. Anything that can be measured will be measured. As the electronic trading infrastructure matured, the pursuit of market inefficiencies became a business of higher and higher frequency of trading. Firms have made this into a "microstructure" effort, searching for intraday movements that identify an imbalance in the supply and demand or an inflection point in the market.

Market data metrics change at every millisecond during the trading session with each and every market transaction. Correspondingly the industry of computerized trading has evolved towards the pursuit of real-time price anomalies. A quantitative investor will take a "micro" view, studying trade by trade in the order book to understand market inflections.

A breakout from a trading range is the most common "signal" that they are searching for. Quants want to understand the imbalances of supply and demand to infer how liquidity changes throughout the day. If they can identify an inflection point that represents the start of an upward trend, they can join the buying and cover the position when the momentum declines (see figure 1.3).

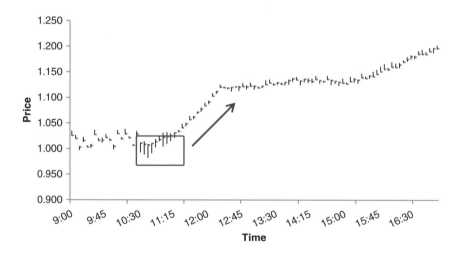

**FIGURE 1.3**   Momentum signals
Note: The price index has been normalized from a base value of 1.0

Correspondingly, for every market rally, there is often a market contraction. A "contrarian" signal attempts to identify the inflection points when a price movement has peaked (or bottomed) and that the market will likely revert to a previous level. If a trader can identify the upward (or lower) price barriers, they can profit off the reversion to the previous price level (see figure 1.4).

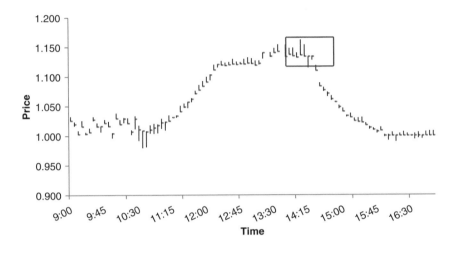

**FIGURE 1.4**   Contrarian signals
Note: The price index has been normalized from a base value of 1.0

Directional movements are not the only domains of price anomalies. The "margin" relationship between correlated securities represents an opportunity to play dispersion strategies. Dispersion represents a perceived price anomaly such as a historically large gap between two otherwise correlated stocks. On an intraday basis, dispersion can result from a price spike in one stock while a highly correlated stock lags the movement. Traders may buy the out-of-flavor stocks against the other, assuming that the gap between the two will revert to previous norms (see figure 1.5).

An "anomaly" only becomes an anomaly when it's irregular, such as a deviation from the norm. The quantitative analyst needs a reference frame to interpret what is within the normal range and what is a discrepancy. The common reference "signals" are volatility, bid–offer spread, and the volume distribution. These are the common denominators that allow the analyst to interpret the strength (or degree) of the deviation.

*Volatility*, the measure of the average change in stock prices, is one of the most important metrics. The differentiation of volatility across stocks is usually a representation of the risk of the asset: riskier

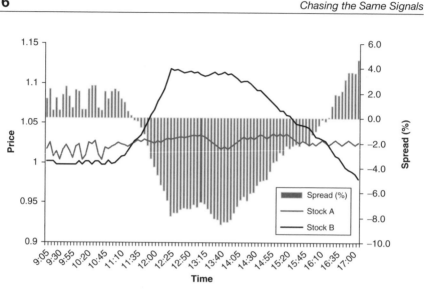

**FIGURE 1.5**   Arbitrage (or dispersion) signals
Note: The price index has been normalized from a base value of 1.0

stocks are assumed to have greater price volatility. Volatility also varies throughout the trading session, because of changes in the supply and demand from investors as well as periods of uncertainty in price movement.

Interval volatility, derived as the standard deviation of a stock's price return from the start of one interval (say 10 minutes) to the next, is a reference for understanding the expected price movement of stock throughout the trading session. A 5 percent price spike is obviously more pronounced in a low-volatile utility company that trades in a narrow price range over several months than a similar movement in a growth stock (see figure 1.6).

*Spread* is the difference between the market's best offer price and best bid price, referred to as bid–offer spread (see figure 1.7). Spread is associated with the costs of trading as it determines the round-trip frictional effects. Tighter spreads are common in liquid stocks where there are depths of investors willing to exchange at the prevailing market price. Larger spreads are more common in smaller capitalization stocks and less liquid securities. The fluctuations in the spread throughout the day are a reflection of imbalances in supply and demand and of periods of greater (or less) uncertainty in where the stock is headed.

*Volume,* the number of shares trading in a window of time, is a proxy for interpreting the relative activity level of a stock. The fluctuations in volume throughout the day can contain information on the sentiments

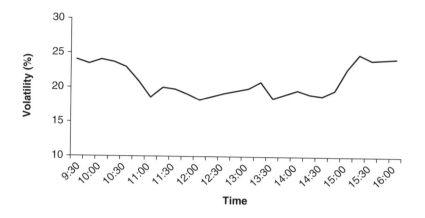

**FIGURE 1.6**    Interval volatility

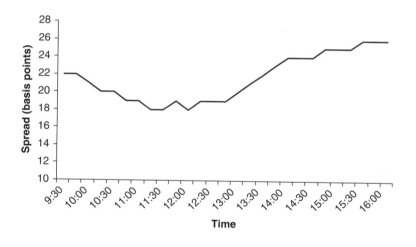

**FIGURE 1.7**    Bid–offer spread

of investors and they are also a proxy for relative aggressiveness of buyers and sellers. Volume distributions are the reference frame for interpreting price movements as in line with historical movements or irregular due to uncharacteristic volume expansion (see figure 1.8).

Although volatility, spread, and volume are only a few of many market data metrics to describe a stock's trading profile, they are arguably the three most common elements to all quantitative investment strategies because they provide a reference for apples-to-apples comparisons across stocks. Quantitative traders are searching

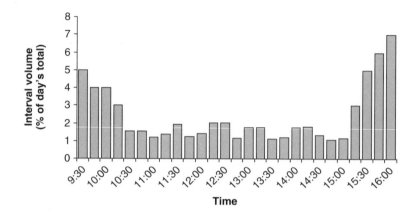

**FIGURE 1.8**   Volume distribution

for "generalized" models that describe the behavior across a broad group of stocks, rather than on an individual stock basis. How is a trader to understand whether a 3 percent price spike compares with a 2 percent price spike in a correlated security?

Quantitative traders "normalize" their signals into common units. They apply their distributions of volatility, spreads, and volume to rank signals into units of standard deviations. They want to quantify that a 3 percent price spike is actually within 1.0 standard deviation of an intraday movement in a small-capitalization stock, while a 2 percent spike is 2.5 standard deviations in a utility company. As a consequence, volume, volatility, and spread distributions have become ingrained as the common metrics that black-box strategies are referencing for their pursuit of price anomalies.

## THE SAME SIGNALS

A casual spectator may wonder whether it's plausible to suggest that all these firms are chasing the "same signals," given that there is a seemingly infinite array of data and unique combinations of trading strategies. The reference to "same signals" is not an implication that all indicators are alike, but rather it's an affirmation of the old expression "there are only so many ways to skin a cat."

It must be expected that there will be a high correlation among signals with the same intention. Momentum, for instance, is case in point of a variable with countless derivations and interpretations: top-and-bottoms, ascending triangles, candlesticks, relative strength indicators, stochastic oscillators, exponential moving averages—all have been profiled in countless technical trading books throughout the years and are available on Yahoo! Finance. They are only the tip of the iceberg in mathematical techniques that broach the vast corners of sciences: neutral networks, fuzzy logic, genetic algorithms, and more.

One firm may have a higher predictive model for momentum but it will have a common relationship with other trend followers—they will be looking at the same stocks, just entering at different times, in different ways, with unique holding periods. However, the byproduct of chasing the same signals is that these strategies will all influence one another.

Disturbances in volatility, volume, or spread are the basic references each firm is monitoring. And as they act on their signals, they influence the marketplace, triggering other computers to get involved. One machine's momentum signal is another machine's contrarian signal. Their longevity becomes a competition for signals, and not just knowing what signals to chase but knowing how to chase them.

Since the publication of the "efficient market hypothesis," there has been endless academic debate on the randomness of stock price movements. The debate will continue; the stock market is always changing, but it is also always the same. The evidence, however, suggests that at least a few firms have been successful in discovering these inefficiencies. At the end of 2008, more than $90 billion dollars were invested with statistical arbitrage and market-neutral hedge funds. More than $40 billion dollars of the world's market transactions are instigated by automated investment strategies each day.

And as a consequence, when one machine is "chasing a signal," it is just as influential to the stock price as the management team announcing a reorganization. The buy-and-hold investors are not forgotten, but they aren't what they used to be.

# CHAPTER 2

# The Automation of Trading

## *When Machines Became the Most Active Investors*

I nvestors are a diverse group of individuals and financial institutions, each with unique objectives and strategies. Pension funds, retail investors, investment banks, speculators, hedge funds, and part-time cab drivers each express unique views and risk preferences as they transact in buying and selling stocks. We assume that markets reflect all these diverse expressions, forming an equilibrium that reflects the "rational" value of the market. We have few insights, however, into the relative activity of the members of each group.

We know that the major holders of the most common large-capitalization stocks are often marquee institutional investors. Fidelity Investments, Capital Research & Capital World, The Vanguard Group, State Street Corporation to name a few, mark the top-10 holders of all most every major corporation in the S&P 500. In the past four decades, U.S. institutional investors have quadrupled their assets to over $10 trillion dollars (see table 2.1).[1]

Although the occasional hedge fund breaks the top 10, the list of major holders by and large is composed of traditional mutual fund managers, who are by nature "buy-and-hold" investors. Mutual funds assume large positions in the stocks, owning several percentages of outstanding shares, and then typically hold these positions for years.

Is it safe then to assume that mutual funds also represent the most active investors in the market place? In a study by academics at the University of Wisconsin-Madison, the trading activity of institutional investors was reverse engineered using the net changes in their quarterly holdings through 13F filings. The results indicated that institutional investors represented only 20–65 percent of total consolidated volume of the Nasdaq 100 index.[2]

Despite being the top 10 in all of the major index constituents, mutual funds were in the minority of investors transacting each day in

**Table 2.1**   Top-10 institutional holders

| Holder | Shares | % Out | Value* |
|---|---|---|---|
| Fidelity Investments | 14,455,947 | 4.58 | $5,031,536,912 |
| Capital Research Global Investors | 11,254,980 | 3.56 | $3,917,408,338 |
| Capital World Investors | 10,740,100 | 3.4 | $3,738,199,206 |
| Barclays Global Investors | 10,446,851 | 3.31 | $3,636,130,959 |
| Vanguard Group | 8,016,563 | 2.54 | $2,790,244,917 |
| State Street Corporation | 7,789,448 | 2.47 | $2,711,195,270 |
| AXA Investment Managers | 5,679,969 | 1.8 | $1,976,970,010 |
| T.Rowe Price Associates | 5,475,892 | 1.73 | $1,905,938,969 |
| Marsico Capital LLC | 4,263,024 | 1.35 | $1,483,788,133 |
| Jennison Associates LLC | 3,700,928 | 1.17 | $1,288,144,999 |

*Source:* Yahoo! Finance

the marketplace. What then is the ecology of the stockmarket, who are the most active investors, and what are their investment objectives?

## THE LEGEND OF DoCoMo MAN

On any typical trading day, a risk trader in Japan trades anywhere in the range of $30–50 million of turnover. He rarely, if ever, carries a position overnight. He only trades in one security, Nippon Telegraph and Telecommunications Corp., otherwise known as NTT DoCoMo (9437.TT). He is a day trader and well known throughout the Japanese financial industry by his alias "DoCoMo Man."

NTT DoCoMo is one of the TSE's most liquid securities, with $200 million of turnover in this stock each day or roughly 1 percent of the TSE's total volume. DoCoMo is Japan's largest telecommunications corporation, with a market capitalization of $70 billion and close to 200,000 employees. The firm provides various kinds of cellular services, including cellular phones, satellite communications, and wireless LANs. DoCoMo Man's interests in the underlying fundamentals do not go beyond its brief business overview.

On any given day, each and every day, DoCoMo Man will time the opening bell of the market and place $100 million of shares on the bid and $100 million of shares at the offer. His orders are triggered to be sent immediately at the opening bell, ensuring more often than not that he's one of the first in the order book queue and will hold priority at his bid and offer price levels.

The order size of $100 million is not arbitrary, it's based on the expected volume in NTT DoCoMo by the natural sellers and buyers.

With an average trading volume of $200 million, DoCoMo Man does not expect his bids or offers of $100 million to be filled any time soon—he actually hopes most of these orders reside in the queue throughout the day. He's trying to own the order book at his price levels and force the street to hit his bids or lift his offers.

This concept of market making is prevalent in all types of distribution businesses. Auto dealers engage in market making when they buy at discount from manufacturers and sell to retail at a premium. They take inventory risk in the vehicles they hold. In the finance world, however, there are limited dealers because of the regulatory environment that prohibits many participants from being on both sides of the market in a single trading day.

Pension funds and traditional mutual funds cannot speculate intraday. Investment banks are closely audited in the risk trading given their conflict of interest managing customer orders. There remain only a few firms with the capital and trading infrastructure to sustain the risk appetite for market making. The barriers create an opportunity.

One of the essential elements to longevity as a market maker is the product demand. A good business demonstrates predictable consumer demand. NTT DoCoMo is a good candidate in that regard because the underlying customers are very stable. There will always be natural flows in NTT DoCoMo because it's widely held by all traditional portfolio managers and pension funds in Japan.

The sheer size of the NTT's representation in the Nikkei225 makes it likely that funds will have daily rebalances to stay in line with the benchmark index. This creates a degree of consistency and stability in the stock's trading patterns. Similarly, it's a public utility stock, so it has low volatility given it's not widely held as a speculative position.

NTT's fundamentals, however, are not the reason for its favorable day trading characteristics—the reasons are related to market structure, in particular the minimum price variation rules of the TSE. The NTT DoCoMo share price is more than ¥100,000, while the TSE mandates a minimum price variance (or tick size) of ¥1,000. At first glance that may not seem excessive, but it's in the range of 0.80 percent for a stock valued at ¥170,000.

NTT is a utility stock and it's unlikely to observe the wild price swings from speculators. This is a company with a stable business and an operating profit of 6–8 percent, so the most aggressive research analysts may forecast an annual price appreciation of 10–12 percent. On a given trading day then, a big movement for NTT may be a 1.0–1.5 percent gain. That means, NTT opened at ¥170,000, traded through

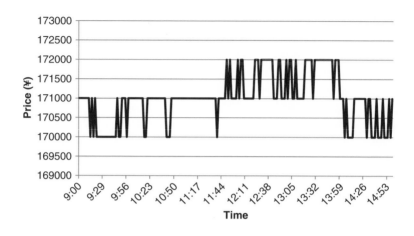

**FIGURE 2.1a**    NTT DoCoMo: intraday price chart

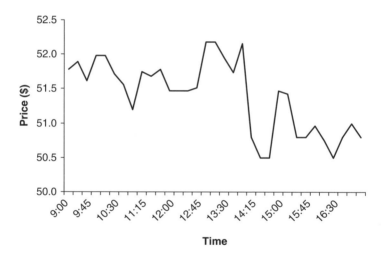

**FIGURE 2.1b**    Amazon.com: intraday price chart

¥171,000, and closed at ¥172,000. A 1.6 percent move but the stock traded at only three unique price levels on the day (see figure 2.1a).

Contrast the market structure with that of Amazon, for which the expected number of price levels is often 20 to 30 prices for a 2 percent gain (see figure 2.1b). The difference between how NTT and Amazon trade is not driven by fundamentals but rather by differences in the market structure. The U.S. markets trade at less than one-cent decimals across several pools of liquidity. The market structure in Japan, by contrast, imposes a single order book with minimum price steps of ¥1,000. NTT will consequently only trade at a few price levels all day for a 2 percent gain.

The priority in the order book is the determining factor in sourcing liquidity. There is a great advantage in being among the first orders on the bid and offer side. If DoCoMo Man is simultaneously hit on the bid side and on the offer side for 1,000 shares, he profits several thousands of yen.

Market making is a game of deep pockets. A trader working small orders into the queue would find themselves behind the institutional flows and would rarely receive fills because of lower priority. To have leverage at the game, a trader must be a substantial portion of the market. DoCoMo Man must be prepared to layer his orders into the depths of the order book, at price levels outside the best bid and offer.

The game of market making works well in trading-range environments in which there is a natural balance of buyers and sellers. In a low-volatility environment, the market maker earns the spread throughout the day, with the ideal scenario having the stock trade within three or four price levels and the ratio of bid volume-to-offer volume balanced.

Transaction costs must be managed. The market maker will accumulate stock if the trading becomes skewed toward one side of the queue, and he may need to quickly lift an entire offer queue and close out an accumulated position. These are the transaction costs of the strategy, which erode his profits. He might make $250,000 over the course of the afternoon session and then give back $70,000 covering the inventory into the market close.

His profits are unpredictable from day to day. In a low-volatility environment, his profits may be more than $100,000 each day. He can give a lot of his gains back quickly, however.

At any given moment, the market can move rapidly against him. DoCoMo Man could get caught out by a sharp market movement on the back of news: the government announces a relaxation of taxes, a Japanese domestic bank announces an adverse earnings report—the Nikkei moves down sharply 2 percent and NTT DoCoMo quickly moves through the prevailing bids or offers.

DoCoMo Man could be hit holding $70 million of NTT DoCoMo and have no sell orders at the new prevailing best offer. If he covers too aggressively, his selling activity may move the stock down another percentage point or more, costing him $1 million. He could retract three weeks of his trading gains in an instant. A few adverse movements could represent a couple months of his trading profits.

He is not ignorant of market fundamentals. He keeps an active dialog with the trading community and attends the occasional morning research meeting. His intention is not to forecast the share price movement but to keep abreast of any unusual circumstances—adverse earnings report, tax reforms, investor sentiment—anything that would make the market erratic. His need for fundamental sentiment is better described as an exercise in risk management.

He didn't learn this craft overnight, either. For more than a decade, DoCoMo Man was employed as a dealer with a large Japanese domestic broker, where he handled client orders for Japan's largest pension funds and institutional investors. Japan has a unique culture within the institutional investment managers—the client is king. If a client specifies an order should be placed at the prevailing bid price, held for three minutes, reduced in quantity by 10 percent and the offer lifted, then repeat until the order is completed—these instructions must be carried out explicitly—and updates are required throughout the day. There should be no deviation from the client instructions and any deviation will be borne by the broker.

Managing client flows is a mechanical exercise, but it does allow one to learn the nuances of the market mechanisms. The TSE suffers a great degree of latency on the cancellation or amendments of orders in the queue—it may take as much as 30–60 seconds to receive a cancellation acknowledgement from the TSE's system, despite the order being canceled within moments of the request.

DoCoMo Man learned to navigate this mechanism; he learned what to expect during spikes in market volume; and he also learned the culture of the institutional client base—how the clients react to market events such as adverse news and price movements. His "rule base" continued to grow.

He also learned key lessons in the regulatory environment. Stock trading, particularly for institutional flows, is a tightly audited activity. Trading too aggressively in a stock may create undue market impact and invite calls from the market's watchdogs. Market manipulation in the form of window dressing brings a heavy penalty in Japan: jail. Appreciation for the unwritten rules of the industry was a practice that had to be incubated over time: a few close calls and the occasional tap on the shoulder and one would learn the boundaries of the acceptable.

It took years before DoCoMo Man could begin to trade on his own account—there are only limited firms willing to provide a trader with

$100 million of capital to play around with each day. He was eventually given the opportunity, and when he generated profits of more than $5 million in his first year, when the Nikkei's annual performance was down 4 percent for the year, he had validated his potential of being a liquidity provider. He was at the beginning of a successful career as a market maker, and he would go on to earn trading profits in the millions year after year.

## COMPUTER-TO-COMPUTER TRADING

In the late 1990s, the SEC introduced a variety of market reforms to improve the efficiency of the marketplace and to encourage the growth of ECNs. Electronic trading materialized through a succession of technologies, industry protocols, and market reforms.

Electronic trading is the ability for an investment firm to route its orders directly to the exchange (or other venue) over an electronic network. Electronic trading is commonly referred to as direct market access (DMA) because the client has the direct ability to execute its orders on the exchange without any manual intermediary, such as a salesperson or market maker.

Electronic trading has a several-decades-long chronology of milestones, and it's still at the early stages of its adoption within the financial industry. In the U.S. markets, it was estimated in 2008 that 35 percent of all trades were initiated by DMA, that is, investors self-trading electronically without engaging a broker. A decade previously, DMA would have been less than 1 percent.

The right to execute an order has historically been a privilege for a minority of designated financial professionals. In the U.S. markets, the *Securities Exchange Act 1934* established the formation of the SEC and new legislation to define the firms with the right to buy and sell securities. The SEC mandated that the employees of "broker–dealers" firms were to be properly licensed before transacting in stocks.

During the subsequent decades after the act of 1934, an investor would need to speak with a licensed coverage representative at a regulated broker–dealer to purchase stocks. An investor couldn't just place its orders with the receptionist, that is. All facets of the order-handling process were under SEC's scrutiny, such as a broker's requirement to maintain an audit trail of dialog with its clients as well as promptly executing their order instructions.

Brokers were the intermediaries necessary for transacting in securities. A designated salesperson would interact with the client to accept orders while a designated dealer (or agency trader) would type the customer orders into an exchange terminal for execution. The execution process was a set of manual steps between market participants, re-entering data into any number of terminals.

The role of the execution dealer was often a unique craft in itself. Not just anyone had the dexterity to perform the function of terminal operator. Most global exchanges had specialized terminals for order entry. Dealers would take years to master the art of navigating the keyboard layouts, which were tailored for local market order types.

One of the initial milestones of electronic trading was breaking away from this dependency on exchange terminals. This process began when financial institutions gathered together to standardize the way in which order instructions could be communicated between counterparts. Orders to buy and sell stocks go through several phases before they are executed.

When an investor calls a broker to place an order, the order will be in a "pending" phase, until sales passes it along to the trader, who then places the order on the exchange. When the exchange acknowledges that the order has been received, the order's phase changes to an "open" state, representing that the order has been placed in the exchange's book but has not been executed. In the institutional investment industry, all these phases an order lives through are important to the investors. For decades, the process to communicate the phases an order passed through before it was executed was manual.

The Financial Information Exchange (FIX) protocol, which was established in 1993, was a major milestone in standardizing the state of an order. Global exchanges had unique ways of describing an order's status. The FIX protocol defined a standardized set of "tags" to represent it. The FIX protocol was an industry milestone for another reason: it allowed for brokers to migrate away from using the exchanges terminals.

Once FIX was available, brokers could connect their proprietary front-end technology to the exchanges electronically and could communicate order instructions by the FIX language. This eliminated the brokers' dependency on the terminal operators and gave them more flexibility in running their trading operations. Brokers could centralize their trading desks, having one group of dealers execute orders across several markets, all from one common front-end platform, rather than several unique exchange terminals. FIX allowed financial institutions to speak the same language electronically.

FIX was the necessary building block to spawn what would become the next generation of execution venues: ECNs. From the inception of Island Inc., the industry's first ECN in 1996, these computerized marketplaces would grow to change the way securities are trading.

## THE LIBERALIZATION OF U.S. EQUITY MARKETS

An electronic communication network is a computerized marketplace that automatically matches buyers and sellers. Unlike the auction-driven markets, Nasdaq and the New York Stock Exchange (NYSE), which necessitated an intermediary to connect buyers and sellers manually, ECNs were completely electronic: when a buyer's order matched a seller's, they were executed automatically.

The origins of the ECN were byproducts of new rules established by the SEC in the aftermath of the October 1987 stock market crash. During Black Monday, when stock markets were plunging, Nasdaq market makers failed to liquidate their small orders from retail clients, focusing purely on the institutional investors. Many retail orders were ignored until the market had fallen significantly. In the postmortem of the 1987 crash, the Nasdaq market structure was renovated to prevent retail investors from being disadvantaged in subsequent market dislocations.

Nasdaq established a new system in 1988, designed to provide retail investors access to Nasdaq execution: Small Order Execution System (SOES). SOES was an electronic order book for automatically matching buyers and sellers, and it was designed for handling order sizes of less than 1,000 shares. The establishment of SOES also mandated Nasdaq market makers to execute retail orders automatically at the prevailing best prices offered to institutional clients.

The impact of SOES wasn't truly felt until the arrival of the tech bubble in the late 1990s because that's when day trading enjoyed its peak of popularity. "SOES houses" began to open in shopping malls throughout the U.S. Anyone with a few thousand dollars could rent a desk and trading terminal that provided a trading platform equivalent to most of the trading floors on Wall Street.

The SOES platform had limitations, however. Since it was designed for small, retail orders, it was not a platform suitable for the institutional investors. ECNs would bring the convenience of an electronic order book to the commercialized level, suitable for institutional clients. The Island Inc., one of the industry's first ECNs, was a sophisticated trading platform. Island designed an electronic order book with improved order-crossing logic and state-of-the-art efficiency. Island was a commercialized platform, capable of rivaling the Nasdaq exchange in terms of speed and order-handling efficiency. Island, along with other early entrants such as Instinet, was ready to compete with the exchanges as an alternative venue for automated execution.

In their early days, ECNs had trouble attracting institutional investors. Since ECNs stood alone from the exchanges, their prices weren't disseminated to all market participants. ECNs often had better prices (higher bids for sellers and lower offers for buyers) but these weren't visible to the institutional investors. Nasdaq market makers initially had no obligation to transact on ECNs or match their prevailing prices.

A turning point came in 1997 when the SEC introduced new order-handling rules in its memorandum for Regulation of Alternative Trading Systems (Reg ATS). The SEC created a formal definition of an alternative trading venue and provided a framework to register and to regulate these new execution venues. The SEC allowed ECNs to decide whether to register as broker–dealers or as national exchanges.[3]

The Reg ATS guidelines imposed subtle rule changes to govern the interaction between ECNs and traditional market-making firms. The "limit order display rule" mandated that specialists and market-making firms should display publicly the better quotes available on alternative trading systems. The second SEC rule, the "quote rule," stated that specialists and market makers should provide their clients with the most competitive quotes.

The two rules in combination would level the playing field between ECNs and traditional market makers. Either venue had to publish the best quotes of the other. And the public was ensured the best available prices at any execution venue.

When Reg ATS was implemented in December 1997, it immediately became a turning point in the uptake of ECNs with institutional investors. The ECN order book would be advertised throughout the traditional market maker's order book. Institutional investors would have access to the vast universe of retail investors and nontraditional market makers.

The environment for electronic trading was maturing, but there was one last leg to truly change the game: computer-to-computer trading. The advent of FIX protocol and ECNs had generated the initial stages of an electronic trading industry but most trades were still conducted over the phone. Although brokers were using ECNs to trade electronically, they were taking orders from clients by manual means.

In 1997, Interactive Brokers would dramatically improve the efficiency of order submission with a new offering: Computer-To-Computer Interface (CTCI). Interactive Brokers was the first firm to allow investors to connect to their systems through an Application Programming Interface (API), that is, a low-level programming language.

The CTCI offered investors freedom from traditional front-end order-entry systems. Clients would no longer need to type an order into a front-end system or use the phone to submit an order. With CTCI, they could connect their own front-end technology directly to the brokers and begin to automate the order-submission process.

For quantitative investors, computer-to-computer would mark the beginning of a new era. Their trading strategies could be automated. Correspondingly, the ecology of the stock market was about to change.

## THE IMPACT OF TECHNOLOGY

Hedge funds eagerly awaited the maturity of electronic trading technology. Despite technological progress not representing a fundamental change to the economic climate, the ability to transact in equity markets without an intermediary, such as a broker or specialist, presented significant opportunities. The prosperity of DoCoMo Man was not a complete mystery to the hedge fund community.

Market making had been a lucrative career for specialists and Nasdaq market makers for decades. Hedge funds were cognizant of the opportunity to get involved, and ECNs were the catalyst. Hedge funds understood that market making was as much a game of mechanical rules as it was instincts. The success of traders was arguably not down to their taking a directional view of the market; rather, they had learned how to react to conditions in the market. They developed rules in response to the "signals" they observed in the markets.

Hedge funds would describe this trading style as "heuristics," in which a set of rules is learned through trial and error. Traders are not completely mechanical; their decisions vary from day to day, but largely their longevity is founded in their practical experience. They learn through doing.

Hedge funds felt they could learn these rules too. And the advent of electronic trading provided an opportunity to get involved, particularly in the layers of securities that were less crowded than the mainstream.

In the late 1990s, market liquidity in Nasdaq stocks was at all-time highs given the lengthy bull market in the technology sector. Microsoft and Cisco Systems were among the most actively traded securities in the world, often trading several hundred millions a day.

Given the activity of technology stocks, their bid–offer spreads (the difference between buy orders and sell orders) were very tight for the most actively traded securities. Spreads always traded at the minimum increments of one-sixteenth of a cent.

But looking down the depth of thousands of securities, the spreads could often be lofty, such as five-sixteenths of a cent. Nasdaq market makers were less interested in these names because there were too many stocks to follow and the action was in the red-hot technology and internet sectors.

Hedge funds realized there would be price improvement opportunities in the less liquid stocks based on economies of scale. Computers could monitor thousands of securities and simultaneously place bids and offers across the entire market. One computer could replicate the activity of an entire room of market makers.[4]

The airlines, utilities, or real estate sectors would be good opportunities. Hedge funds could dabble in market making with improving the prevailing bid–offer spread, capturing as much as two-sixteenths or three-sixteenths of a cent per trade. A few thousand dollars a day could be earned in a single name. They were engaged in a similar game as the professional Nasdaq market makers, offering liquidity to the market and capturing spread for taking risk.

And hedge funds believed they would eventually have the upper hand on the traditional market makers. Their rule base would continue to evolve, learning various trading scenarios and devising more and more intelligent strategies for managing risk. The business was ideally suited for mathematically inclined professionals to devise models for maximizing profits.

They would seek to learn these mechanical strategies through research, in areas where other investors rarely ventured: the order book. They would study the mechanics of the order book, changes in bid–offer spreads, intraday ratios of buyers to sellers, the frequency of upticks to downticks, the velocity of trading—it would be a new way of looking at the markets.

Regardless of the fundamentals of the underlying companies, much could be learned about the stock from observing its trading patterns at a "micro" level. A dramatic imbalance in bids in the market represented upward pressure on the share price. A sudden absence of trades on the offer side clearly represented a reversal.

Hedge funds also had a significant advantage over individual traders. Rather than trading individual stocks alone, they could distribute risk across several hundred or thousands of stocks. If they were getting hit in a particular stock that was moving downward, they could cover in a correlated stock and hedge out the market risk. They could apply the latest innovations of portfolio theory to the age-old business of market making.

As the hedge funds began to play the game of automated market making, they began to learn the many pitfalls and nuances that our friend DoCoMo Man had learned. Market latency, system outages, volume spikes, and limit-order imbalance brought a lot of uncertainty to the optimization problem. Much logic, or trading rules, needed to be introduced to their models.

If futures move down sharply, they might cancel all outstanding bids and cover 10 percent of their portfolio at market immediately. If the frequency of changes in the order book increases to the offer side, cancel all outstanding offers. Success at the game became the ability to navigate the market mechanisms, to understand the limitations and the practical side of order submission, cancelations, and amendments.

The hedge funds took this business to a new level. All those live tick data feeds broadcasted throughout the trading session could be archived and used as a resource for back-testing their trading logic. With a historical database, hedge funds could pore over the data and understand trading patterns, and estimate sensitivity of spreads to earnings announcements, news reports, and index movements. It would be a scientific approach to market making.

The SEC would continue to augment its market reforms and improve the efficiency of the marketplace.[5] The markets would observe the influences of spreads and corresponding reduction in costs of trading. Hedge funds too would become more creative in their strategies and more competitive in their investment in technology.

"Black-box" trading, as it became known, began to grow in prominence in the marketplace. From 2000 to 2005, the usage levels of DMA, the portal to electronic trading, would grow from inception to represent more than 30 percent of all U.S. market turnover. The average product spreads on Nasdaq stocks reduced from 30 basis points (0.30 percent) to eight basis points (0.08 percent). The number of people working on the floor of the NYSE would be reduced from 3,000 in 1999 to fewer than 1,200 by 2007.

Computerized traders had arrived on Wall Street and had cannibalized traditional market makers.

## A SYSTEMATIC INDUSTRY

Since the inception of ECNs, computerized traders have blossomed into an influential source of market liquidity. In the decade from the adoption of Reg ATS in 1997, they had grown to represent a third of all market transactions in the U.S. markets. They have evolved from simple rule-based trading to the most highly sophisticated of portfolio strategies ever.

Our conventional view of the stock market is that of a barometer for the economy. The health of our economy is reflected in the prevailing highs and lows observed throughout the day. We hold that public policy, entrepreneurship, and scientific innovation are the driving forces behind our economic prosperity.

On any given day, however, some of the daily gyrations in the markets are governed by a minority of participants that are completely agnostic to the long-term sentiments of politicians and economists. They prefer to specialize in knowledge of the market structure and the mechanisms that connect buyers and sellers.

In our systematic era, the daily highs and lows are largely influenced by the competition among black-box strategies, each expressing unique risk preferences and objectives as they navigate the market mechanisms.

The industry has undergone sweeping changes on the back of the advancements in electronic trading platforms. Whether floor traders in the Chicago Mercantile Exchange, NYSE specialists, or Japanese dealers—quantitative firms have entered the domain of traditional participants—and often cannibalized their livelihood. Consequently, the ecology of the marketplace has migrated away from traditional mutual funds and industry insiders such as DoCoMo Man.

Black-box firms have been pioneers in many regards, being among the first financial institutions to adapt ECNs and to analyze unique data sources for their investment strategy.[6] It has been a learning process throughout, capitalizing on the prevailing market conditions and adapting to the marketplace. It hasn't been without pitfalls, as they too have learned—change is inevitable. The only true "optimal" objective is survival, and to survive, they must adapt.

DoCoMo Man too learned much from trial and error. He evolved over the years, becoming extremely proficient at market making, and had a record year in 2007 with profits of $25 million. His good fortunes, however, came to an untimely end just less than a year later—and it wasn't subprime or credit related.

In July 2008, the TSE, in an effort to improve the efficiency of the marketplace and to attract foreign capital, reviewed its market structure and decided to reduce its minimum tick size for stocks priced greater than ¥100,000 from ¥1000 to ¥100.

For NTT DoCoMo, this meant a reduction from an 80 basis points spread to an eight basis points spread. The market rules that had ensured a narrow price trading range of two or three price steps were eliminated and so was the ability to own the order book at any price level.

The Japanese marketplace had evolved. And DoCoMo Man was last seen crying into his sake.

# CHAPTER 3

# The Black-Box Philosophy

## *Why the Best Hedge Funds Don't Attend Conferences*

E very year in September, investment professionals from the world's top investment firms are invited to attend one of the industry's most individual and exclusive investor conferences, it's hosted by an independent Asian research firm known as Credit Lyonnais Securities Asia (CLSA).

The CLSA conference is an annual event held in Hong Kong, featuring 1,000 of the world's top fund managers and 500 company executives. The conference line-up and agenda are what makes it unique and sought after by the industry's elite money managers. The CLSA line-up brings together a colorful assortment of thought-provoking topics and forward-thinking industry leaders, not to mention rock and pop icons from the 1970s.

At the 2007 CLSA conference, the headline speaker was Bob Geldof, the former lead singer from British rock band The Boomtown Rats and world-renowned political activist for the eradication of African poverty. From the time he launched the 1985 LiveAid concert, Geldof had pursued a lifelong campaign to raise awareness of ongoing starvation in Africa nations and the policies that maintained their plight of poverty. Geldof had spent most of 2005 on a year-long study of Africa's problems, deemed the "Commission for Africa," initiated at the request of Tony Blair.

He was uniquely qualified to address CLSA conference's attendees on the economic, political, and geographical problems in Africa. He was also uniquely qualified to comment on the investment opportunities that would arise from a coordinated global effort to increase international aid, foreign trade and the standard of living in Africa over the coming decades. That is why he made a good candidate as headline speaker; investors were searching for an understanding of the long-term potential for the public markets in African nations, in addition to a chance to rub elbows with the stars.

CLSA has made a name for itself as a unique research boutique that strives for differentiated investment research.[1] The firm is renowned for looking at a broad picture and seeking out investment themes for the long term. Bob Geldof is only one of many unique speakers who have been featured at CLSA's conferences over the past two decades.

A recent conference featured one of the world's foremost genetic scientists, who presented findings on the potential for genetically engineered earthworms to solve the world's global warming problem through an engineered digestive system that consumes carbon dioxide emissions. The research breakthrough might be years away, but investors were keen to understand the nuances of this process and the likelihood of its commercialization in the coming years.

A prior CLSA conference featured a heated debate between an Israeli terrorism expert against a Palestinian militant over the future of the Gaza Strip. The debate was a unique platform for investors to understand better the historical rifts between the two groups, the current environment, and the likelihood for stability in the next decade. Investors cannot easily infer the influencing factors of political stability from their research publications alone. By attending conferences, the industry's elite money managers can formulate a more informed sense of the economic climate and political trends.

Professional fund managers at the large investment firms, such as Fidelity, Wellington, Putnam, and American Century, have access to many resources for analyzing investment opportunities. Fund managers may attend 10 or 20 investor conferences over a year, ranging from the macroeconomic styles of CLSA's conference to sector-specific topics such as cancer research, Vietnamese banks, or Las Vegas gaming companies.

Throughout their conferences and business trips, value investors might meet with as many as a couple hundred senior executives, whether CEO, CFO, or CIO, at the corporations they are evaluating. The large funds receive substantial access to corporate management because they often have the capacity to assume a substantial position in the company.

A firm such as Fidelity has the clout to be the largest institutional holder in a variety of large-capitalization stocks, whether McDonald's, Microsoft, or AT&T. The sheer size of the institutional funds awards them access to top management. After earnings announcements a fund manager could expect to receive a personalized walkthrough of the earnings results from the CFO. On any given day if there were adverse news or rumors, the fund manager could readily have the CEO on the phone for his or her commentary.

Fund managers also have teams of analysts to provide the detailed analysis of balance-sheet metrics against their valuation models. In addition to their own internal analysis, institutional investors use sell-side research analysts a lot. They are constantly reading the latest research publications and discussing investment theses with their various industry contacts.

However, all the research reports and corporate management access are insufficient to prepare for adverse market events. Even the elite money managers, with all their analyst teams and macro advisors, were ill prepared for the economic tsunami that would transpire during the fall of 2008.

In late September 2008, a few days after the conclusion of CLSA's investor conference in Hong Kong, global markets began to observe a global market correction. The Dow Jones Index would plunge 30 percent over the span of the next few weeks, as would comparable global indexes such as the DAX, Footsie, Hang Seng, and Nikkei.

Emerging markets and currencies were the hardest hit as investors reduced their risk preferences for the security of U.S. treasuries. There was no sector to withstand the market correction. Utility stocks that had years of stable earnings reports were also thrown into a tailspin during the chaos. The market was effectively observing a "revaluation" across the board.

Value investors were among the worst-performing funds in 2008, most were observed to post 40 percent declines on the year. Most marquee investment firms behaved like deer in the headlights. Warren Buffett's Berkshire Hathaway would lose 38 percent of value in 2008, mirroring the declines in the Dow Jones.

Although success stories in 2008 would be few and far between, there would be a category of hedge funds that held their head above water during the market turmoil. This group of hedge fund managers did not attend the CLSA conference, nor were they even on the invite list of the prestigious event. They had not met with a single CEO or CFO over the course of the year, nor were they privy to personalized phone calls after earnings announcements. No one walked them through the financial statements because they were agnostic to traditional research. This category of hedge funds is known as black-box investors, and they would weather the global financial crisis better than their peers.

The top-performing hedge fund in 2008 would be Renaissance Technologies, a firm based on Long Island, Connecticut, founded by James Simons in 1986, a Ph.D. in mathematics, and notorious for hiring mathematicians, astrophysicists, and computer scientists to design and manage its array of black-box strategies. Renaissance would post a 58 percent return for the 2008 year, consistent with a 20-year track record of double-digit returns.[2]

In November 2008, Simons would be requested to speak to the U.S. House Committee on Oversight and Government Reform on his views on the financial crisis and the contribution of hedge funds to systematic risk in the global markets. While commenting on the origins of the financial crisis, Simons would describe his firm Renaissance Technologies as an "atypical investment manager."[3]

The best-performing hedge fund in 2008 didn't recruit MBA graduates, it didn't subscribe to sell-side equity research, and its fund returns had no correlation to the market's direction: the epitome of atypical.

## THE MARRIAGE OF SCIENCE AND ECONOMICS

Quantitative investors have always been an obscure community of investment professionals. There are few similarities between value-based investors and black-box investors, if any. Quantitative investors are looking at everything that is measurable, while traditional investors are looking at that part of the business that is not measurable. These firms differ in all aspects of their investment process from how they determine the valuation of stocks to how they implement their investment strategies, to the culture of their businesses.

Traditional investors want to understand the intangible aspects of a company such as its brand, management ability, and corporate strategy. The quality of these aspects is not always best understood by reviewing the company's balance sheets. Starbucks, for instance, was founded on its vision "to inspire and nurture the human spirit." If investors had compared it to another coffee franchise by its balance sheet alone, they would have missed out on one of the biggest success stories in history. Traditional investors are searching for firms run by management like Howard Schultz, with both the vision and ability to build a global franchise.

Traditional investment research is predominately a qualitative undertaking. Investors want to understand the broader economic picture and then determine what stocks are the best investments within that region or sector. Political stability, regulatory environment, foreign restrictions and taxation, currency appreciation or depreciation, and demographics are all macroeconomic issues that influence the formulation of their investment sentiment. They wish to interpret the macroeconomic climate before they begin to scrutinize the balance sheets of underlying corporations in those regions.

Once an investment theme is identified, they then look at the best stocks in that particular sector or region that are positioned to grow. They scrutinize balance sheets, corporate strategy, consumer trends, and competitive edge and then build a portfolio based on the best assets value for money. Sell-side (i.e. investment bank) research analysts, CFOs, and corporate insiders are their primary resources.

Empirical analysis may be used to complement the portfolio managers' investment ideas, but most of their decisions are based on qualitative factors. They ask questions such as what part of the business cycle is this industry facing? Is this a strong management team? Do this company's products have a strong brand? Do the consumers in their demographic have disposable income? They wish to understand how the stock's earnings will perform in a six-month-to-18-month (or longer) horizon and whether stocks are priced fairly based on their judgments of earnings potential.

Quantitative investors, conversely, are agnostic to subjective factors. They are not concerned with the quality of the corporate management or the uniqueness of the mission statement. Quantitative investors prefer to labor in the details of the stocks' transaction histories. They compare Starbucks to McDonald's, not by the products they sell, but by the volatility and liquidity of their share price movements.

Quantitative investors are focused on an entirely different economic problem. They are not concerned with a long-term view of the market or the overall economic climate. They are concerned with understanding the process of how investors interact and how that manifests itself in a stock's trading performance in terms of volatility, liquidity, and spread. Quants are agnostic to the overall valuation of the market.

They want to understand whether imbalances in supply and demand are the result of investors' risk preferences; whether the market structure influences the volatility of the stock; whether investor behavior has any characteristic biases. These are the factors that materialize in "price anomalies" and the patterns of market activity that are not random fluctuations.

Quantitative investors are concerned with the broad nuances of the stockmarket's behavior. Do changes in analysts' ratings influence the share price? Do value stocks outperform growth stocks in periods of market distress? Why do stocks that have underperformed the market tend to rally in January? These are the questions that "econometric" professionals ask themselves.

## Econometrics

*Econometrics* is the application of statistical methods to the study of economic theory. These economists are searching for "price anomalies" that arise based on economic consequences. They want to understand how changes in accounting practices will affect the future earnings performance of stocks; how changes in interest rates will influence the valuation of the markets; how the taxation rates affect the consumer price index.

Econometricians formulate an empirical model around a fundamental economic theory and quantify the statistical significance of relationships among economic variables. They ask themselves questions such as why do stocks with low price-to-earnings (P/E) ratios tend to outperform high P/E stocks over a 10-year horizon? Why do closed-end funds appreciate toward their net asset value in December? Why do value stocks outperform growth stocks during recessions? What's the impact of macroeconomic news announcements on the volatility of the stock?

Econometric models are generalized themes that quantify the statistical significance of technical indicators at forecasting movements in a stock's share price, volatility, or liquidity. These models are formed on sound economic theories and intuitive concepts; the mathematical models allow economists to measure the merits of the theory and to quantify the relative value of one stock against another.

## Microstructure Research

*Microstructure* research, by contrast, is a much more detail-oriented analysis of how stocks are traded. Equity market microstructure research is an emerging field of economics, growing in prominence over the past decade. It is the science of studying the role that market mechanisms play in the process of price discovery. These economists want to understand how different order types, rules of transparency, dissemination of information, and auction mechanisms influence how stocks are traded. That is, do different market mechanisms lead to differences in a stock's average spread, volatility, or liquidity?

Microstructure research has important significance to black-box firms because it's central to understanding the execution process. This research allows quantitative firms to determine what is the best way to implement their trading strategies. They want to understand how to minimize transaction costs relative to execution benchmarks, such as vwap or the market open; how to execute a $1 million order and incur the least amount of market impact; whether its advantageous to suspend trading when bid–offer spreads are wider than their historical average.

## Optimization and Execution

*Operations research* (or numerical optimization) complements the microstructure research process. Black-box firms apply optimization methods for a variety of objectives: to minimize transaction costs during their strategy's execution; to minimize the concentration of risk across thousands of stocks; to minimize the correlation with the index movement. Numerical methods are the tools that quantitative investors apply to maximize their trading profits.

*Technology* is arguably the most essential competency of any black-box strategy. Regardless of the quality of their empirical models, quantitative firms must ask themselves whether they have the capacity to execute their strategies. Can we trade thousands of stocks a day? Do we understand the latency of the market mechanisms? Can we achieve priority in the order books?

The most successful black-box firms all have one thing in common: state-of-the-art execution platforms. Their technology allows them to participate in market rallies, to hedge risk in real time, and to capitalize on short-term price discrepancies. Without technological prowess, they couldn't stay one step ahead of their peers in the marketplace.

Many fields of science are applicable to understanding the stock markets: fuzzy logic, expert systems, neural networks, and pattern recognition to name only a few. Although quantitative firms may apply different empirical methods, they must ask themselves the same basic questions: what macroeconomic ideas are driving price discrepancies? Do we understand the market structure? What's the optimal way of implementing our strategies? Do we have the technology to gain an edge?

Black-box firms can therefore differ along any layer of that thought process, some being better at devising econometric models, while others are more capable at executing thousands of orders each day. Each depends on the ability to marry science and economics and to exploit an edge over the investment community.

The overall economic climate is less relevant for black-box firms than for traditional investors. The expression "the rising tide lifts all boats" does not apply to black-box firms. Quantitative investors prosper on their ability to understand the nuances of the market structure and to implement strategies that capture short-term inefficiencies. Black-box investment strategies are the lubricants in the financial markets, feeding on the interactions between buyers and sellers.

## THE CULTURAL DIVIDE

Measure, manage, and model are the staples of the quantitative investment industry. While traditional investment managers prefer to spend their time engaging corporate management teams, political advisors, and research analysts on the latest in earnings outlooks, the quantitative investment firms are accumulating data to model the earnings history in terms of volatility and momentum.

One of the overwhelming differences between the fundamental investment community and the black-box community is their treatment of traditional sell-side research. A survey by Greenwich Associates, an independent research rating organization, estimated that mutual funds spend upward of $6–$8 billion of commission dollars each year to acquire U.S. research products from investment banks. The full suite of research is inclusive of written research publications, contact with research analysts, and active sales coverage. A top-tier mutual fund is likely to have 200 or more sales and research coverage staff dedicated to its global account.

The pitfalls of sell-side research are well known and have been documented in many industry studies. During the peak of the tech bubble, a query of sell-side research highlighted that 75 percent of analysts' recommendations were "buy." Studies have confirmed the natural tendency of analysts is to be overly optimistic on the outlook for a particular stock. The analyst's relationship with the corporate management makes it difficult to author a negative report on the stock. A "sell" recommendation can be adverse to the relationship and to attracting investment-banking business.

But despite all the known pitfalls of sell-side research, traditional managers still spend billions of dollars a year to acquire it. Furthermore, industry surveys suggest that less than one-third of all mutual funds have implemented any form of systematic process to quantify the accuracy of their research coverage. Billions of dollars in research, yet no attempt to determine whether it's good research or poor research. But in 2002, a quantitative hedge fund in London decided to apply "measurement" to this industry of sell-side research and they became one of the industry's most profitable hedge funds as a result.

Marshall Wace, one of Europe's largest hedge funds with $15 billion in assets under management, has achieved much of its success through an innovative process that combines qualitative and quantitative research analysis. In the first few years from its inception in the late 1990s, it relied on traditional stock selection methods. In 2002, it decided to incorporate a quantitative process to measure the quality of sell-side research. The result was a proprietary system called "Trade Optimized Portfolio System," or simply TOPS, as it is now known throughout the industry.

The essence of TOPS is a broker survey to collect stock picks across the industry of research analysts and equity salespeople. Each morning sell-side sales and research professionals throughout the industry will log on to Marshall Wace's system and register their best ideas for the day.

Marshall Wace doesn't accept phone calls from brokers. It wants to standardize its interactions with sell-side professionals to "measure" the quality of its recommendations. Each morning, sell-side professionals are mandated to enter their ideas into Marshall Wace's TOPS. Just as they would call a client to discuss their opinions, sales interact will communicate with TOPS to record high-conviction ideas, buy or sell recommendations, market-timing views, and long-term and short-term forecasts.

The system allows salespeople to specify a single stock (or combination of stocks), the direction and target holding period, their target entry and exit prices, and any comments. The system will maintain a daily profit and loss statement, and sales is able to close a position ahead of its target holding if it changes its view.

The TOPS algorithm will aggregate all the survey information and quantify the proficiency of the sales professionals. The algorithm is designed to measure what people are good at, such as whether they are good stock pickers or good at market timing. Do their research upgrades (or downgrades) lead the markets or are they simply trend followers? Each sales contributor is ranked for proficiency at generating money-making ideas.

TOPS will then build a portfolio of long and short positions based on the most proficient contributors. Its survey includes thousands of contributors throughout the industry but only a small fraction of the contributors' ideas will be implemented in its portfolio.

The idea behind the TOPS strategy is very intuitive and a sound business case. The financial industry is filled with hundreds of equity sales professionals, who dedicate 12 hours per day to reviewing and scrutinizing their firm's equity research. Of the hundreds of professionals, Marshall Wace believed that some would be savvy at stock selection, consistently picking winners and losers. By measuring the sales within its system, it would infer who had the most consistent ability.

By implementing this TOPS process, Marshall Wace effectively outsourced its internal portfolio management to the brokerage industry. Rather than build its own team of research analysts to make investment decisions, Marshall Wace used the entire investment community to contribute to its investment process. Its systematic approach to stock selection removed much of the emotional element around investing. It did not buy into the story of the day or the latest piece of research, but rather quantified a broad group of contributors and based its investment decisions on the consistency of these professionals.

Marshall Wace endured a few years of teething to implement its unique process. It was obviously a very big distinction for sales to log ideas into a system, rather than just speak directly with a fund manager. But there was much incentive for brokerage sales staff to participate in the TOPS survey: Marshall Wace shares profits with the brokers that generate revenues for its firm. Its equity commissions are allocated to the brokers who contribute to its fund performance—in much the same way as traditional long-only fund managers rank brokers, but the Marshall Wace process is designed to eliminate any emotional basis. Sales professionals that make money are rewarded with a share of the profits. It was an incentive-based system and it works!

TOPS is better described as a "hybrid" strategy and an automated black-box strategy, although it remains a systematic process. Marshall Wace recalibrates its algorithms from time to time based on discretional views of the market environment. It is also challenged with attrition of its contributors given that analysts move from firm to firm, change jobs, and leave the industry. In excess of 20 percent of their contributors change from year to year. The system is consequently very dynamic, evolving over time.

Marshall Wace's innovation with TOPS effectively introduced a new paradigm of accountability into the financial industry. Brokerages had never measured the proficiency of their analysts' stock selection because evaluating distribution business had historically been a subjective process. Clients rank sales proficiency based on subjective topics such as intensity of service, access to analysts, or timeliness of calls. Marshall Wace proved to the industry that by introducing a systematic process, an investment strategy could be very profitable. It also proved that if there are no metrics, there is considerable incentive to go out and measure for yourself.

## Measure, Manage, and Model

The distinction between traditional investors and quantitative investors goes well beyond the differences in their investment strategies and their research process. The disparity between the two food groups also encompasses both their culture and their belief system.

Scientists, by nature, have an inherent need to "measure, manage, and model." They have little appreciation for subjective opinions or intangible research. Their investment strategies revolve around a hypothesis and its supporting research.[4]

There is certainly more glamour in traditional investment research. Global firms are often built on the strength of their CEO's charisma as well as the strength of the business plan. Traditional investors view their role as a "partner" of the corporation, working alongside the industry's management to achieve long-term growth.

The concerns of quantitative investors are deemed trivial details of the long-term investor. Whether stock's short-term volatility is increasing or decreasing is not an issue for the traditional investor. Whether the market structure influences the width of the bid–offer spreads is not a factor for the investor planning to hold for at least three-to-five years.

The black-box investment strategy is better described as a "philosophy." An investor is either a believer or a nonbeliever; the short-term movements in the markets are random or they contain patterns; trading technology is a revenue center or just a cost of doing business; execution proficiency is determinant of top-tier fund performance or it's a commodity across all funds. Choosing which camp one belongs to is rarely a conscious decision.

## THE BLACK-BOX COMMUNITY

Renaissance Technologies is one of the longest-standing quantitative hedge funds since being founded in 1986. Apart from Renaissance's 58 percent return in 2008 and its average double-digit annual returns from inception, there is little public information about this firm. Quantitative hedge funds are a secluded community.

Most black-box firms shy away from the lights of Wall Street, preferring more tranquil environments such as Long Island, Milwaukee, Des Moines, or Santa Fe. Their executives do not attend the high-profile investor conferences, nor are they sought after for market commentary on CNBC financial newscasts.

The success of their privacy is in part a luxury of the lack of interest in their investment strategies. The traditional investment community would deem their strategies as incomprehensible science. Terms such as fuzzy logic, fractal methods, and genetic algorithms are not engaging to the community that prefer investor conferences and dinners with the likes of Bob Geldof.

As the black-box phenomenon has evolved, so too has the interest in these firms. Many quantitative fund managers have been among the highest earners in the financial industry—Jim Simons, David Shaw, Cliff Asness, Monroe Trout, Peter Muller—and their success has attracted much attention. One of the more prevalent commonalities observed among black-box firms is their distinctive culture. These firms differentiate themselves from traditional asset managers in that they reflect a strong academic foundation. D.E. Shaw, one of the industry's flagship statistical arbitrage firms, was not only a pioneer in quantitative trading, but was also an incubator of the quantitative "brand."

David E. Shaw, a Ph.D. in computer science from Stanford University, became known for his firm's rigorous recruiting policies, which especially targeted the math and science majors. The staff of D.E. Shaw included multiple Rhodes scholars, international math olympiads, Putnam winners, national chess champions, and other world-renowned researchers. Effectively, D.E. Shaw branded black-box firms as the "rocket scientists" of finance.

The rocket scientist mantra has its shortcomings. Few investors have ever become interested in the inner workings of their strategies, in part because of lack of interest but also because of the nature of quantitative firms. These funds guarded their models as though they were a new pharmaceutical drug pending a U.S. patent protection. Quantitative traders became notorious for their privacy.

Their privacy was a byproduct of a unique dilemma to their peers in traditional asset management: intellectual property. If other black-box competitors employ a similar strategy, the short-term discrepancies they are chasing will begin to decay. The plight of a black-box firm is a continual effort to identify, exploit, and maintain profitable trading opportunities. When they find these successful strategies, they must guard them for themselves as long as possible.

As a result, the inner workings of their black-box investment strategies are held close to the chest. Quantitative funds have a culture that is notorious for protecting their prized models. The "signals" that their algorithms monitor to initiate their buy/sell decisions may be known to a small inner circle of senior executives within the firm. They do not engage in market commentary and are not likely to divulge performance figures, apart from disclosure to their core investors.

Although it's not uncommon for hedge funds to be private about their trading strategies, quantitative hedge funds have an extra layer to the dilemma. A black-box strategy is a set of formulas, embedded in a computer language. And any trader or analyst could potentially walk away with their prized models. A successful statistical arbitrage strategy or trading algorithm might take years of research and millions of dollars of risk trading to develop. All of that "proprietary research" could easily walk out the door if an employee were to copy the algorithms onto a floppy disk.

Quantitative managers are often paranoid about this flight risk. One solution to protect their intellectual property was the "noncompete" agreement. The basic structure of a noncompete arrangement inhibits employees from leaving to start their own fund or to join a competitor for a set period, anywhere from one to three years. Noncompetes may also contain clauses to mitigate risk further: restrictions on soliciting investors of the fund, working with former colleagues, or corresponding with any of the firm's feeder funds. These contracts may also forbid employees from having lunch with one another.

The noncompete arrangements were only the tip of the iceberg in the effort to mitigate proprietary risk of attrition. Quantitative firms would structure their teams in concentric circles, minimizing the interactions among different business functions and inhibiting knowledge sharing.

It was consequently unlikely to see any of their research professionals attending the marquee investor conferences hosted by CLSA.

The longevity of a black-box firm, such as Renaissance and D.E. Shaw, is not only a function of its investment process but also a testament to its distinctive culture.

## THE COMING OF AGE

Quantitative hedge funds have been among the best-performing funds in the industry over the past decade. They have achieved double-digit returns throughout various economic cycles. Whether in the U.S., Paris, or Tokyo market, black-box trading has come of age in the past decade.

The growth of assets invested with black-box trading has largely been based on their returns. In particular, quantitative hedge funds have been among the best in fund performance measured by risk-to-reward. The Sharpe ratio, the measure of fund performance coined by Nobel laureate William Sharpe, ranks the quantitative funds as the highest quality of investment strategies.

The Sharpe ratio is derived from the fund's mean return divided by its standard deviation of the return, thus evaluating the fund's return in units of its risk. A fund with volatile returns ranks low in performance quality. The top-tier funds have posted Sharpe ratios in excess of 3.0 over the past decade, suggesting that their annual returns are exceptional relative to the risk required to achieve those gains. A firm such as Renaissance, for instance, may generate an average return of 2 percent a month with few (if any) months with losses.

The performance of black-box firms is also believed to be uncorrelated to the market. That is, their returns are independent of the market's direction. They can make money equally in a bull or bear environment, provided that the market's volatility and liquidity are sufficient. This strikes true to Simons' comment to the U.S. Congress that "his firm has little correlation to the market."

The growth of assets invested with quantitative hedge funds was no surprise given that they were generating double-digit returns with little relationship to the market's direction (see figures 3.1 and 3.2).

An academic research study estimated there were more than $160 billion of assets invested with quantitative hedge funds at their peak in 2007. There were more than 600 hedge funds that described themselves as quantitative investors.

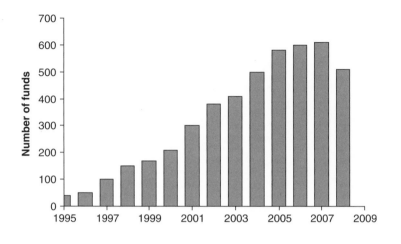

**FIGURE 3.1**   Growth of black-box funds

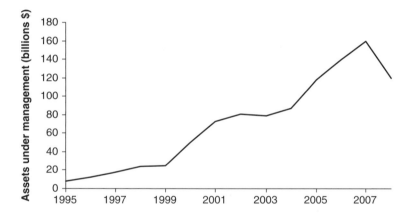

**FIGURE 3.2**   Assets under management of black-box funds

What is also transparent is the footprint that black-box firms now cast in the global equity markets. They are estimated to be more than 30 percent of the daily turnover on major markets such as the Nasdaq and NYSE exchanges, the LSE or Japan's TSE.

They are correspondingly one of the driving forces behind the proliferation of ECNs. These automated crossing networks have the black-box funds to thank for their livelihood. Renaissance is suggested to be as much as several percentage points of Instinet's daily turnover alone. The black-box community paved the way for the widespread adoption of ECNs in the U.S. markets, and a global theme seems to be developing with the sprouting of ECNs in Europe and in parts of Asia.

Despite representing only a fraction of the $1.3 trillion hedge fund industry, black-box firms are the predominant liquidity providers in the marketplace. And, as evidence suggests, the wake of their trading models creates a tide from Wall Street to Shanghai.

# CHAPTER 4

# Finding the Footprint

## *What Coke and Pepsi Do Not Have in Common*

T he efficient market hypothesis has been one of the most widely accepted theories in finance for the better part of three decades. It asserts that stock prices trade based on all known information and they adjust instantaneously to new information. Stock prices trade along a "random walk" and fund managers cannot make excess returns when trading on news, earnings announcements, or technical indicators.

Efficient stock markets are best characterized by how they react to new information. Stock prices should react instantaneously to the new information—the distribution of their returns should reflect a normal distribution (i.e. the standard bell curve) around the release of information—some stocks go up and some down.

Similarly, in efficient markets, stock prices should not demonstrate serial correlation, the relationship between one period and the subsequent one. Yesterday's prices are not indicative of today's prices. If stocks were up one day, there should be no correlation to predict a positive movement on the next. The fluctuations day to day in stock prices should be randomly distributed.

There are many published academic studies that highlight periodic anomalies. Most research, however, indicates that few investors could act on the anomaly because of frictional effects (commissions, clearing fees, taxes) and market restrictions (short-sell constraints). Academics often suggest that anomalies are rarely stable enough to form the basis of a trading strategy.

In the case of the black-box industry, the debate on the efficiency of the stock market should not be viewed as a discredit to their business model, but rather as a byproduct of their business. They are one of the main reasons markets are efficient.

## STATISTICS AND ARBITRAGE

Central to the belief in market efficiency is that "informed investors" drive stock price movements. The trades of informed investors convey information that causes a persistent impact on the security price. The magnitude of the price impact is held to be a function of the number of informed investors relative to the population of investors. In an efficient marketplace, the arrival of new information should be the catalyst for moving a stock from one price level to the next.

Any casual observer of the stock market will note that stock prices appear to "oscillate" throughout the day; a trendy +3 percent market movement usually doesn't occur in one large step, but rather in successive ups and downs, slowly gravitating to a new level. Every stock chart is riddled with fluctuations of price jumps and reversals: these oscillations are most often the result of "imbalances" in the urgency of investors.[1]

Imbalances are momentary disproportions in the number of buyers and sellers. Investors demanding too much liquidity in a period will cause an imbalance in shares available for trading and will create an impact on the market. Imbalances are a regular occurrence in stock trading given the diversity of investors' information, objectives, and risk appetites. Whether it is caused by greed, fear, or ignorance, an investor that demands too much liquidity will move the price of a stock.[2]

Price movements that are not driven by informed investors will often not cause a sustainable impact on the share price. The stock will revert to its previous level once their buying (or selling) has been completed. These momentary disturbances are measurable by the degree of "serial correlation" in time series; the price movement in one period is inversely related to the subsequent period (also known as mean reversion).

Even Eugene Fama, the founder of the efficient market theory, has recognized that markets that might be quite efficient over a daily horizon might not have completely unpredictable returns from trade to trade and minute to minute. Efficiency doesn't just happen instantaneously. On an intraday basis, investors often require time to absorb new information, and markets will oscillate until the investment community has reached an equilibrium.[3]

Empirical evidence supports that the many global stock markets have a greater intraday variance (open-to-close) than an overnight variance (close-to-open). In an article published in the *Journal of*

*Finance* entitled "Stock Return Variances: the arrival of information and the reaction of traders," economists quantified that the hourly stock price movements were 10 times more volatile during market hours than when the market is closed.[4] There are various schools of thought on this behavior: investors may overreact to new information; or informed investors transact on their knowledge too aggressively. Another hypothesis is that public information arrives during market hours more frequently than when markets are closed.

One of the most common intraday anomalies is known as "inverse autocorrelation," in which stock prices are said to be mean reverting. A study conducted by microstructure professors at the University of Southern California (UCLA) illustrated this market behavior for NYSE-listed securities. Their research validated that overnight stock returns are serial independent while the intraday movements are less efficient (see figure 4.1).

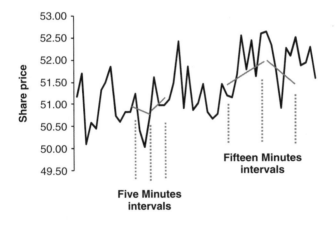

**FIGURE 4.1**   Analysis of serial correlation

On a five-minute interval, NYSE stocks demonstrate an inverse serial correlation: stocks that move up in a five-minute window more often than not will revert in the next five minutes.[5] The investment strategies that are confirmed with understanding these intraday correlations are known as "statistical arbitrage" (or high-frequency) traders.

Statistical arbitrage firms devise mathematical models to quantify order imbalances and to understand the affiliated market behavior. This type of high-frequency trading is a form of "liquidity provider" in that by chasing small price anomalies it is offering liquidity to stabilize imbalances. It is an investment strategy as well as an influential liquidity provider.

## THE LAW OF LARGE NUMBERS

High-frequency trading encompasses a very broad group of trading strategies that target intraday price anomalies. Their models will target momentum, mean reversion, lead/lag, or spread opportunities and will have holding periods of anywhere from hours to a few minutes. The only commonality between trading strategies should be their foundation of "statistics" and "arbitrage."

Statistics, by definition, imply that an empirical model was applied to describe the probability distribution of price anomalies. Whether using a traditional linear regression approach or a more elaborate application of the physical sciences—pattern recognition techniques or neural networks—the trading strategies must be founded on a formal mathematical process.

Arbitrage denotes that the strategy is based on a short-term discrepancy, formed from a historical reference. Although an arbitrage strategy typically denotes a simultaneous discrepancy between two (or more) securities, in the context of statistical arbitrage it represents any deviation from an expected value. The expected value is derived from the historical reference of stock's microstructure profile such as volatility, liquidity, or spread.

The most intuitive representation of a statistical arbitrage strategy is a "mean reversion" strategy, in which the model is targeting the relationship between two or more correlated securities that are subject to the same set of risks. In an arbitrage strategy, an investor buys one stock and shorts against a similar stock, attempting to profit from the change in margin between the two assets.

Coke and Pepsi, for instance, although different brands selling to different demographics, will share the same risks with respect to costs of raw materials, labor, inflation, and consumer preferences. As a byproduct of shared risks they will move inline with the overall trend of the consumer beverage sector. A mean-reversion strategy will take positions when the "price gap" between Coke and Pepsi deviates from its historical range by a statistically significant distance. The strategy might buy Pepsi and sell Coke, if there were an intra-day price spike of say 3 percent between the two. The model is suggesting that Coke is overvalued relative to Pepsi in a statistical sense.

Fundamental investors also employ mean-reversion strategies between similar stocks. They are in the business of valuing stocks and they will simply buy the ones they like and sell the one they don't like. The reality, however, is that the intraday price disparities are usually ignited by supply and demand imbalances, rather than changes in prevailing fundamentals. A quantitative trader attempts to segregate the "informed" market movements from the noise and then participate in oscillations that occur in absence of news or events.[6]

Statistical arbitrage trading suffers an image problem due to the unfair affiliation with "technical" trading. Technical analysis is the usage of charts or graphs to support an investment thesis. Although there is some commonality with quantitative analysis, charts say very little about statistics or arbitrage.

Technical analysis arguably evolved to support the effort of marketing securities. It's common to read through a fundamental research analyst's investment thesis and find a chart to support the recent consumer growth, raw material costs, or demographic changes. Charts provide a language to reinforce the key economic drivers within the investment thesis (see figure 4.2).

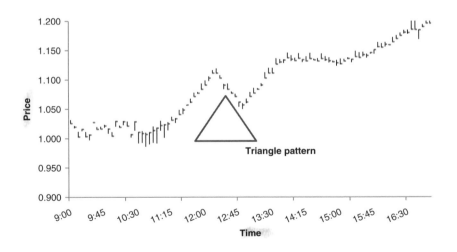

**FIGURE 4.2**   Technical indicators
Note: The price index has been normalized from a base value of 1.0

Similarly, there is a rich library of "technical indicators" based purely on historical price trends; triangle patterns, head-and-shoulders, double bottoms, candlesticks, and many more names are given to a variety of patterns that can be visualized. These all have their merits but shouldn't be confused as the basis of a multibillion-dollar industry of black-box trading.

High-frequency trading strategies are derived from "generalized" models that quantify the statistical significance of price anomalies across a broad range of stocks. A generalized model incorporates thousands of historical observations that are available to quantify the significance of generic anomalies. Although a valid argument could be made to suggest there are individual differences in how stocks trade (i.e. Amazon.com to American Airlines), generalized models offer much greater potential because they can distribute individual risks by trading hundreds of stocks.

If a traditional hedge fund were trying to play the relationship between Coke and Pepsi, for instance, they would suffer from exposure to a variety of risks. Coke and Pepsi, despite all their similarities, are far from perfectly aligned in their business operations. They are large, global conglomerates with many different parts. Coke may have a large bottling plant investment in Mexico, subject to the movements of the Mexican peso. Pepsi, alternatively, may have larger operations in South America, influenced by a host of emerging-market risks.

A union strike in Costa Rica could easily result in a sharp sell-off of Pepsi and perhaps even increase asset allocation toward Coke. A $10 million long position in Pepsi, hedged with a $10 million short position in Coke could easily wind up with both sides losing money. The investor's intention of hedging against the risk might well have been more costly than an unhedged position.

High-frequency strategies are thus intended to participate in hundreds or thousands of stocks, preventing exposure due to unforeseen risks in a particular stock or sector. The development of generalized trading models is based on "time series analysis," in which an array of discrete time buckets are formulated at regular sampling intervals; archives of five-minute (or shorter) samples of trade price, midpoint, volatility, volume, and other factors across an entire asset class.

Quantitative firms can then manufacture their trading signals by determining statistical relationships between adjacent periods: positive correlation between successive time intervals denotes trend-following opportunities while negative correlation represents a reversal (or mean reversion) opportunity.

Using five-minute intervals of NYSE stocks would create millions of interval samples in a single year of data. When applied across a longer history, there are vast resources to develop generalized models. If a high-frequency firm can identify an indicator with even a small predictive significance, it has the foundation for a profitable trading strategy. The concept is based on the law of large numbers, in that a small marginal correlation could represent shifting the odds in your favor.

One of the longest-tenured high-frequency hedge funds was quoted as having only a 51 percent accuracy of making money on a trade. It just so happens that it earns more profits when its forecasts are correct than it loses when its forecasts are wrong.

## INSIDE THE ORDER BOOK

Technology increased the opportunities for statistical arbitrage firms. As the efficiency of electronic trading evolved, the industry of statistical arbitrage firms migrated from trading at discrete intervals (five-minute windows) to trading in real time. The area of quantitative research that evolved to explore these types of anomalies became known as "microstructure" research.

Microstructure research is concerned with understanding the intermediation of trading when buyers and sellers transact. It is the science of understanding how differences in the market structure (costs, market mechanisms, transparency, dissemination of information) influence how investors reach the equilibrium of price valuation.

In the past decade, microstructure research has been a rapidly growing field of economics given the widespread availability of data sources and improvements in data-mining technologies. These new age economists concern themselves with questions such as does a decrease in minimum tick size (i.e. one-eighth of a cent to one-sixteenth of a cent) improve the liquidity in the marketplace? Does a closing auction reduce the end-of-day price volatility? Is there any correlation between volume of shares trading and price reversals?

Microstructure research is concerned with understanding the minutest changes at the "order book" layer of trading. The order book represents the sequences of events that transpire during a trading session, the most commonly known are the sequence of bid, offer, and trade quotes. Even a casual investor is familiar with the traditional ticker tape information; bid price, offer price, last trade price, and daily trading volume.

| SYMBOL | BID | ASK | LAST | VOLUME |
| --- | --- | --- | --- | --- |
| XYZ | 55.0 | 54.2 | 54.3 | 12,000 |

A more micro view of the order book reveals a continuous sequence of events, representing each change in the book's content. When an investor places a buy order at the prevailing best bid price, the order book reflects the increase of shares on the bid. When a trader crosses the spread to lift an offer, a trade occurs at the prevailing offer price, and the corresponding shares are the last trade size disseminated to the market. Every sequence of changes in the order book represents a new event and each event is broadcasted to the market place (see figure 4.3).

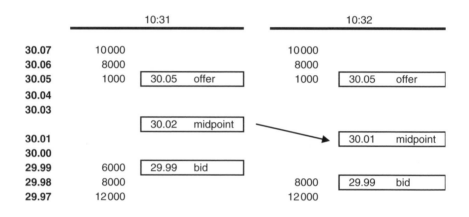

**FIGURE 4.3** Order book analysis—changes to the midpoint

Microstructure researchers compile a vast array of interesting "micro" variables to better describe the composition of the order book and to interpret the interactions between buyers and sellers (see table 4.1). If 20,000 shares traded in Microsoft, there is much more

**Table 4.1** Microstructure variables

| Microstructure variable | Definition |
| --- | --- |
| Midpoint | The difference between the bid and offer prices |
| Bid volume | The number of shares traded at the bid price (seller initiated) |
| Offer volume | The number of shares traded at the offer price (buyer initiated) |
| Bid-to-offer ratio | The ratio of bid volume to offer volume, also known as the "money flow" indicator |
| Effective spread | The difference between the last trade price and the midpoint price, times two |
| Weighted bid price | The average of all bid prices weighed by number of shares at each depth |

that can be inferred than simply the most recent volume. If the shares traded on the offer price, the buyer is assumed to have initiated the transaction; if the volume of shares was significantly greater than the previous transactions, new information may be flowing into the market; if the total shares available now on the offer side are now less than half the bid side, there is an imbalance in the order book.

The order book provides the richest level of information for analysts to understand the imbalances of supply and demand. Imbalances, arguably, are not random events but regular occurrences. An imbalance arises because an investor demands too much liquidity in a period. If there is new research out on the stock, or if there is a key macroeconomic announcement in the sector, an investor may have a heightened urgency to change its position on a stock and has a willingness to create market impact.

In the absence of news or research, investors may still regularly demand more liquidity than the market can bear. The most prevalent reason is the sheer size of institutional investor holdings relative to the market. Institutional investors are among the largest holders given their assets are a substantial proportion of available market capitalization. When a portfolio manager at a mutual fund changes weightings on the stocks within their portfolio, even a subtle change such as increasing their position in Google from 3.5–3.6 percent can translate into a huge demand for liquidity.

Institutional orders flows are predominately "block" transactions in the range of $10 million or $20 million dollars. It's common for institutional investors to trade 30–40 percent of the day's volume in particular stocks when portfolio managers are rebalancing their weightings. As institutional managers are jostling around in the market, their trading activity manifests into subtle "signals" that they are in demand of liquidity.

These signals are visible only at the order book layer; the volume of shares in a window of time grows by multiples of the previous window; the time between successive trades in the market increases frequency; the ratio of transactions on the bid side versus the offer side skews in favor of the imbalance. Microstructure research is a process of identifying these "footprints" in the market.

In recent years, there have been a variety of research studies into the inefficiencies that occur at the microstructure layer. One form of inefficiency suggested by Hans Stoll at Vanderbilt University is known as "inventory effects."[7] If markets had perfect liquidity, the bid price and the offer price would remain in a stable range supplying unlimited liquidity to the buyers and sellers; prices would only adjust to new information arriving. But in the practical marketplace, bid–offer spreads oscillate because of the unique preferences of participants, uncertainty in the marketplace, and imbalances between supply and demand.

An implication of inventory effects is that prices would demonstrate reversals following "quote" changes because trades create a momentary distortion in inventory available. Their research into the inventory effects revolved around understanding how movements in the "midpoint," defined as half the distance between the bid price and the ask price, influenced the subsequent price movement. They wanted to quantify whether a trade that occurs on the bid side (i.e. seller initiated) and correspondingly moved the midpoint lower, was likely to result in a successive transaction on the bid side.

Based on the evidence by Stoll, order book transactions are not entirely random. High negative serial correlation during changes in the midpoint is observed frequently in their analysis. A large buy order (which raises the market's midpoint) is followed more often by a sell order than another buy order.

Microstructure research has many layers of creativity, given the vast amount of available data for research. The sequences of trade activity often lend insights to the sentiments of the market participants: a rapid increase in trading volume can denote an inflection point; a brief window of successive upticks are observed, followed by a price gap of several price depths. Researchers are studying these sequences of order book movements to understand better the future movement in the stock price.

One of the more intuitive ideas revolves around "money flow" indicators, defined as the difference between buyer-initiated trades (called upticks) and seller-initiated trades (downticks). Money-flow indicators are a simple way of inferring the money entering or leaving a market. If a trade occurs on the offer side of the market, the buyer must have initiated it. If on the bid side, the seller must have initiated the transaction. The difference of volume of upticks and downticks is a proxy to infer whether money is entering or leaving the market.

In an article appearing in the *Journal of Finance* entitled "Can Money Flows Predict Stock Returns?," researchers highlighted the strong evidence of "money-flow momentum" in NYSE stocks.[8] If uptick trades are assumed to be buyer initiated, a positive bias on the uptick volume corresponds with "excessive demands" of buyers and consequently drives the stock higher. Stock price movements are strongly influenced by the momentum of money-flow trends. By analysis of the order book, in the author's view, an investor can formulate a short-term prediction on the movements in the stock.

Statistical arbitrage firms, however, are the minority of investors that have the capacity and the expertise to put microstructure research to good use. A few years archive of historical intraday tick data is well beyond the scope of the average hedge fund, let alone institutional investor. A sample of one month of the Nasdaq 100 index stocks would represent hundreds of millions of transactions!

The infrastructure to support statistical arbitrage research is an expensive proposition. Quantitative research analysts require archives of upticks to downticks, rate of change in the order book, average trade sizes, frequency between successive trades, and so on. And since there are exhaustive ways of modeling the order book, the demand for data resources is equally exhaustive. The proliferation of high-frequency firms has correspondingly been a game of few entrants.

## A GAME OF MILLISECONDS

As the frequency of trading gravitated from hourly holding periods to real-time trading strategies, their demands for efficiency had a ripple effect throughout the industry. High-frequency firms have been the most prevalent asset managers in their demands for efficiency at every layer of the execution process; brokerages' trading technology, data vendors' real-time price feeds, and stock exchanges' platforms.

Statistical arbitrage firms have correspondingly introduced competitive pressure throughout the food chain of equity trading. They have raised the expectations for stability and quality of data vendor feeds. They have pressured brokers year-on-year to reduce their commissions for DMA services. They have inspired exchanges to improve their market structure to attract new investors.

One of the more compelling contributions of their influence is that exchanges have recently begun to offer a new service known as "co-location" hosting. This service is offered to asset managers who wish to eliminate an unnecessary intermediary in their execution process: the broker. Co-location is a hosting service in which asset managers can run their algorithms on computer servers that reside at the stock exchange's data center.[9] This service minimizes the "latency" in the execution process.

Latency is the time it takes to submit an order and to receive an acknowledgment. It's analogous to the time it takes to dial a phone number and have the person answer. For long-term investors, this is a technical detail that they rarely would consider a factor in their investment process. For statistical arbitrage firms, latency can be the main difference between chasing a signal and catching it. If seconds of latency can be reduced to the millisecond range, a firm can have a significant edge on its competitors.

Nasdaq recognized the importance of latency to high-frequency firms. In 2005, it was the first exchange to begin offering "co-location" services and within one year it had more than a dozen clients enrolled. Co-location was a natural progression in the maturity of electronic trading technology. As electronic trading had matured, the service of electronic trading brokers could be characterized as nothing more than a pipe to connect to the exchanges.

The pipe, however, is a bottleneck because client orders had to pass through all the broker's order validation and risk management systems. These extra layers of checking offered little value to those wishing to trade into and out of the market as quickly as possible. Co-location provided a solution for the high-frequency clients to eliminate one hurdle in the food chain. The exchanges had incentive to offer the hosting services because they received monthly fees for access and usage.

By co-locating, an asset manager could get its trading algorithms to reduce the transaction speed from seconds to milliseconds. The difference in latency can mean the difference in capturing the small margins. As an executive at Trillium Trading, a high-frequency proprietary trading firm that co-locates at Nasdaq, puts it: "You get proximity to Nasdaq's matching engine, which is important. The margins for profit are thin, so anything you can do to eliminate slippage due to geographical latency helps. When one of the automated strategies sees a change in the marketplace and wants to react, we get the first bite on the wire."

By designing state-of-the-art execution platforms, the statistical arbitrage firms are able to maintain an edge on their competition, chasing the same signals just a hair quicker than their peers. This has allowed many to maintain a high performance level and to sustain profitable strategies in light of increasingly competitive markets.

The demand for speed has had a knock-on effect throughout the financial services industry. In 2007, Thomson Reuters, the industry's largest provider of real-time stock-price data, embarked on a novel approach to reporting earnings announcements. Rather than have research analysts pore over companies' earnings releases and write a brief note to interpret the results, Thomson Reuters created "Robot Reports" to write earnings reports and blast throughout the financial community in milliseconds.

The Robot Reports employ algorithms to interpret the earnings results and disseminate them automatically to the investment community. Within an instant of a company releasing its earning statement, the Robot Reports will tell investors whether the results were "average" or were "excess" earnings. The reports are brief and lack commentary, but they do convey the essence of the earnings results in the blink of an eye.

The industry has truly evolved into a game of milliseconds. Perhaps what's most interesting is that the most active asset managers (based on turnover, not holdings) are arguably the least knowledgable about the fundamentals of the companies they trade. Its not uncommon for a high-frequency trader not to know the names of the stocks they trade. Descriptions aren't important; rather, they are fixated on the symbol, volatility, spread, frequency of order-book updates, and every other microstructure statistic imaginable.

## LIQUIDITY PROVIDERS AND MARKET EFFICIENCY

The debate on the randomness of stock prices is likely to be timeless, attracting opinions from the best and brightest academics and active investors. In his best-selling book, *A Random Walk Down Wall Street*, Burton Malkiel eloquently addresses criticism from the industry's most prominent academics from the emerging fields of financial engineering and behavioral finance. He responded to a variety of publications by prominent academics such as Andrew Lo, Richard Thaler, and Craig MacKinley. Malkiel depicted their contradictory evidence as "potshots" on the efficiency of the marketplace.

Some of the more notable anomalies discussed are the "January effect" where small-capitalization stocks advance in the first week of the year because of taxation; the "hot news" response, in which rallies are observed after surprise earnings; the "initial P/E predicator" where stocks with low P/E consistently outperform the market after 10 years; and so on.

While Malkiel acknowledges the contradictory evidence, he describes the anomalies as "statistically loose." In other words, any of the price discrepancies are too small to compensate for frictional effects of trading, such as taxes and commissions. In his opinion, "no one person or institution has yet to produce a long-term, consistent record of finding money-making, risk-adjusted individual stock-trading opportunities, particularly if they pay taxes and incur transaction costs."[10]

High-frequency firms, if anything, have been successful in pushing friction costs down to historical lows. After the birth of electronic trading, brokerage fees began to wear away year on year at the most rapid pace in the history of the equity markets. Brokerage commissions had historically been priced across the full suite of brokerage services, inclusive of research, sales coverage, corporate access, investment conferences, and execution. Electronic trading (or DMA) commission rates, however, were priced independent of all the bells and whistles of traditional investment research; it was an "execution-only" option for investment managers, and the initial commission rates for DMA were about one-third of full-service commission rates (see figure 4.4).

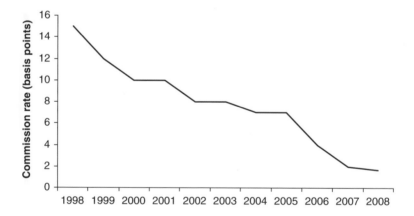

**FIGURE 4.4** Commission rates of DMA

Year on year, the competition for winning the electronic trading business of high-frequency asset managers accelerated the competition between brokerages. By 2008, the realized commission rates for the elite black-box trading firms would be less than a fraction of a cent per share for U.S. equity trading. The "frictional" effects of trading had declined to one-fortieth of the levels observed a decade previously.

Consequently, the economics for high-frequency trading has changed year on year as the frictional effects have become less pronounced. Price anomalies that skeptics might have assumed were unable to cover the costs of trading have become tangible. High-frequency firms have been able to chase price anomalies that are only observable to the trained eye.

The true costs of trading go beyond the fixed commission rates. Market impact is the bigger contributor to cost. Market impact is the market-price movement that occurs from the time of making a decision (i.e. a signal) to the time of executing the order. It is the largest source of frictional cost, particularly for high-frequency firms, and it can be the key determinant of a profitable strategy.

By that token, statistical arbitrage is a practitioner's game, because the market-impact costs can only be learned from actual trading. Backtests and simulations are only useful as proxies, but they cannot be deemed indicative of actual trading results. As a firm acts on a particular signal, its trading will influence the market and thus erode its ability to capture that signal.

In their book, *Optimal Trading Strategies*, Robert Kissell and Morton Glantz refer to the friction effects of trading as the "Heisenberg Uncertainty Principle" of finance because it's impossible to know the price impact had an order not been submitted to the market. The true costs of implementing a high-frequency trading strategy are only known after the fact. By trading, a firm influences the signals that it chases.

Statistical arbitrage firms must learn by trial and error. As they implement models, they learn whether five-minute "margins" are tangible or whether 10-minute holding periods are necessary to cover frictional costs. They gain actual market-impact statistics from their trading and then can fit those costs back into their models, recalibrating and refining their models. The proof is ultimately in the pudding, regardless of what their skeptics believe.

Despite all the contradictory views on the efficient market hypothesis, there is one overwhelmingly consistent opinion on the marketplace: it's constantly changing. Academics and practitioners agree that widely known anomalies have a tendency to disappear, either due to traders attempting to exploit them or due to dynamic changes in the environment.

Academics Richard Roll and Avanidhar Surbrahmanyam at UCLA have also highlighted an important trend; market efficiency is not static over time. From 1998 through the mid-2000s, the intraday efficiency of NYSE-listed securities had improved. Their research demonstrates that "serial correlation" of NYSE stocks has been on a steady decline for most of the past decade. The decline accelerated in the late 1990s when electronic traders began to flourish and then further accelerated when decimals were introduced in 2001. Those five-minute windows of serial correlation have decayed to a fraction of their statistical significance (see figure 4.5).

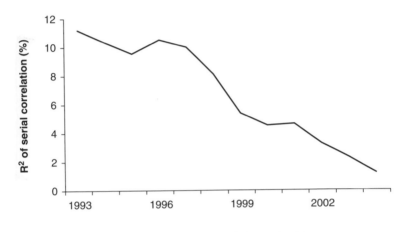

**FIGURE 4.5** Decay of serial correlation

This market trend is not fuel to the fire of the skeptics of high-frequency trading; rather, improvement in the market efficiency represents the contribution of the statistical arbitrage industry. By providing liquidity during periods of imbalances, market efficiency has improved. Higher liquidity, supplied by statistical arbitrage traders, has increased the degree of intraday efficiency of the NYSE.

The growth of statistical arbitrage over the past decade has benefited the investment community through lowering the prevailing frictional effects of trading. In the absence of high-frequency firms, investors would bear transactional costs through greater intraday volatility, imbalances and bid–offer spreads.

High-frequency liquidity providers have been offering a stabilizer role in the marketplace. They are rewarded with small profits off tiny margins, and are only a success because of executing thousands of transactions each day. Consequently, they now cast a large footprint in the marketplace themselves.

In an article appearing in *Business Week* entitled "The Most Active Trader You Don't Know," Steve Cohen's SAC Capital was estimated to represent 3 percent of NYSE's daily turnover alone.[11] Other majority statistical arbitrage firms such as Renaissance, Citadel, and Highbridge Capital have similarly been noted for their excessive level of turnover; some estimates have suggested they turnover 100 percent of their assets every three or four days.

A handful of black-box firms thus generate several billion dollars of high-frequency trading each and every day in U.S. markets; as much as 10–15 percent of total turnover. At this massive level of trading activity, even when commissions have declined to fractional cents per trade, a firm would be insolvent within weeks (or less) if it was unsuccessful in capturing profits from intraday discrepancies. Black-box firms are not outside the efficient market hypothesis; rather, they are liquidity providers that deliver market efficiency.

# CHAPTER 5

# Disciples of Dispersion

## *Why Some Investors Don't Read Fundamental Research*

One of the reasons black-box firms have always been an iso- lated group within the financial community is their treatment of fundamental research. They just don't want it.

The attitude of dismissing the importance of fundamental research is a prime contributor to the alienation of "quants" from the rest of the financial community. It's simply an unsettling disposition from the view of traditional investors because it contradicts their conventional wisdom. Fundamental stock analysis, in their view, is the staple of picking the right stocks. Good companies are founded on intangible qualities: the strength of their management teams; the quality of their business plans; their ability to execute amid economic challenges. Fundamental analysis is necessary to interpret these intangible traits.

There is no greater sentiment on the importance of fundamentals when considering "microcap" companies. A microcap stock is broadly defined as any publicly listed firm with a market capitalization of less than $250 million. The vast majority of U.S. stocks are microcap by that definition. Of the Russell 2000 index, which represents 98 percent of the U.S. market capitalization, over half are microcap stocks.

Microcap firms represent some of the most lucrative investment opportunities. Discovering a stock at its infancy can result in massive share price appreciation. A thousand-dollar investment at the early stage can grow to millions of dollars if the company's business turns out to be a hidden success story. Even casual investors like to search for these opportunities, whether it's an emerging gold mine or the latest state-of-the-art renewable energy source. The lucrative upside potential of small companies presents a lively game in itself.

Microcap stocks are notoriously risky. Given their size, they have less stringent reporting requirements and many do not file quarterly earnings statements. The SEC has looser regulatory requirements for small firms, and it's not uncommon to observe cases of fraud. Even the best firms may simply fail to execute on their business plans and go out of business during the slightest hiccup in the economy. Fundamentals, in many investors' view, play an influential role in determining a successful venture. Investors, consequently, should give the risks careful attention before dabbling in microcap stocks.

Quantitative firms, alternatively, are also very active in microcap investing. But they approach investing in this sector without digesting every piece of available research. Many of these black-box firms hold their positions for several years, equivalent to their peers in the fundamental community.

Quantitative investors value research; they just happen to value a different type of research than fundamental investors. They ask different questions than traditional investors. They form economic theses that affect how a collection of stocks will trade, rather than on an individual firm basis. Their research is known as econometrics, the application of statistics to economic theory, and it has led to some interesting trading strategies.

## ECONOMETRIC RESEARCH

Investors have often commented that there are great differences in the quantity of research analysts covering microcap stocks. Some firms have a dozen analysts, while others have none. Despite the attractiveness of microcap stocks, the available information on small firms differs greatly across the sector. Research is often limited to whatever is published on the companies' website and whatever is discussed within internet chatrooms. Similarly, your local stockbroker may know a story or two on the company but have little (or no) "professional" analysis of the company's earnings and balance-sheet history.

Although a firm might be an exciting startup offering the latest nanotechnology for waste management or offering an innovative biomedical treatment for impotency, there will be few if any investment bank analysts that publish reports on the stock. The reason is that sell-side research is highly skewed toward large-capitalization stocks because they have greater liquidity and have greater commission opportunities.

Investment banks that produce equity research typically align their research coverage with the capitalization of the market. Since banks do not have infinite resources to cover all listed securities, they attempt to capture as much of the market capitalization as feasible with their research teams. For this reason, analysts' coverage tends to crowd around the large-capitalization names; there are roughly 60–80 dedicated analysts for the largest-capitalization firms such as General Electric or McDonald's. Further down the food chain, there are usually 10–20 research analysts on the tail end of the index constituents.

In U.S. markets, the largest firms by market capitalization average 30 research analysts per stock. The bottom tails of the S&P 500 stocks have seven-to-10 research analysts. For the mid-range firms that have market capitalization of between $100 million and $500 million, the average number of research analysts is fewer than 10 (see figure 5.1).

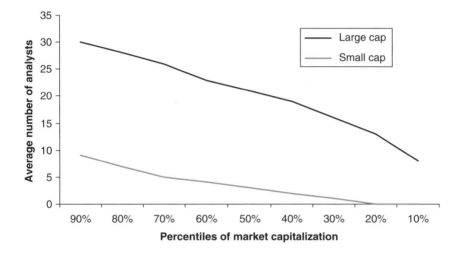

**FIGURE 5.1**   Research analysts by size of firm

In the Russell 2000 index, which represents 98 percent of the U.S. market capitalization, there are more than 400 stocks (21 percent) without any dedicated research analysts. Emerging startup ventures, despite how attractive they might seem, might not receive analyst coverage until there are signs of life in their earnings results.

Economists have wondered whether there are any noticeable effects in the way a stock trades because of the number of research analysts. Are stocks with more analysts more efficient, for instance? Does the number of analysts affect the flow of information to investors? Are there any noticeable lead/lag effects based on number of analysts covering the stock?

There are numerous fundamental economic reasons the number of research analysts would translate into different trading effects. Regular research publications on a stock are highly affiliated with marketing by investment banks, which mobilize their sales and distribution teams to market the analysts' research publications. Banks make more noise on a stock when there are more publications to market.

Formal research also helps a small firm establish its brand. With analyst coverage, the firm's management team will field meeting requests from mutual fund portfolio managers and will receive invitations to industry conferences. Microcap firms have more opportunity to penetrate the institutional side of the financial community with more formal coverage.

Economists believe, in particular, that it's plausible for earnings information about microcap firms to get out more slowly than large firms. Reason being, there are fewer analysts covering these firms and thus less individuals to disseminate information. The theory is that stocks with fewer analysts take a longer time to convey firm-specific information across the investment public.

The economic concept is known as the "gradual information diffusion" theory, which suggests that firm-specific information, especially negative information, diffuses only gradually across the investing public and manifests in predictable momentum effects. If true, the momentum opportunities, in microcap stocks, would be asymmetrical with respect to good news and bad news; that is, economists would expect to observe stronger negative momentum effects in the losers' stocks. This trend would validate that bad news—loss of key customers, declined patent application, and so on—would be diffused to the investment community slowly.

Market efficiency with respect to gradual information diffusion is exactly the research that economists at Stanford University set out to validate.[1] They investigated the momentum effects of U.S. stocks for a 16-year sample period and concluded that there is a strong relationship between momentum effects and the market capitalization of a stock. During their sample period, smaller-capitalization stocks outperformed the market on a six-month horizon by an average of 1.43 percent per month (17 percent annually). Large-capitalization firms, however, observed no momentum effects, which suggested that information was disseminated efficiently to the investment public.

Looking closer into the momentum effects led to further insight: they found that the bulk of the momentum in the small firms was attributable to the loser stocks. Stocks that had underperformed the market had much further downside in the next six months. This supported the researchers' hypothesis that "bad news travels slowly"; when small companies have bad news, their management have little incentive to disseminate to investors, so the information greatly lags the market, that is, travels slowly. Think of a firm that has no analyst coverage and is sitting on good news; the company's management are likely inclined to push the knowledge out the door themselves proactively through public disclosures or announcements. Contrary, consider the situation of sitting on bad news: its managers have little incentive to bring investors up to date quickly.

By further segregating the smaller firms based on number of analysts, they deciphered an interesting explanation in the momentum effects. Momentum and number of analysts were highly negatively correlated. Fewer analysts meant greater momentum. On average, the firms with the fewest analysts (1.5 analysts per stock) had roughly 60 percent stronger momentum than the stocks with the most analysts (9.7 analysts per stock).

This market "inefficiency" research had strong implications for a profitable trading strategy, which the researchers at Stanford proposed as a "momentum-neutral" strategy. In a microcap portfolio, buy the firms with little coverage and sell the firms with more coverage. In the 16-year sample period, this strategy achieved an annual return of 8.4 percent. And by buying and selling an equally weighted portfolio of these microcap firms, they could outperform the market with little exposure to the movements of the index.

What the study on momentum-neutral shows is that investors can realize profitable long-term investments without a detailed understanding of the company's fundamentals. No need to review research publications or read the latest news. No need to understand the intricacies of their technology or to speculate on a pending patent approval. Two factors alone—momentum and number of analysts—are sufficient to earn profits in microcap stocks. This is the power of econometric research.

Econometric research is a merger of statistics and economic theory. These economists are searching for "price anomalies" that arise due to economic consequences. The research is often intuitive and the anomalies can be explained by fundamental reasons. Econometric research is the cornerstone of one of the largest segments of hedge funds: market-neutral investment strategies.

The broad appeal of market-neutral funds allowed the black-box industry to penetrate the institutional investment community and to grow into one of the largest segments of hedge funds. Market-neutral firms were offering an innovative research process that was founded on sound economic principles. In doing so, quantitative hedge funds would offer an attractive proposition for traditional investors: the ability to make money in bear markets.

## MARKET-NEUTRAL STRATEGIES

In the late 1990s, alternative asset strategies (or hedge funds) would begin to grow in popularity. Investors, particularly the high net worth individuals, were beginning to feel that the U.S. equity market valuations were unrealistically high on the euphoria of the new age internet stocks and they were beginning to search for alternative investments as protection against a potential correction in the markets. There was strong demand for alternative investments strategies that were unrelated to the overall market movements. Investors were looking for "alpha"—funds that could make money regardless of the direction of the overall market.

"Alpha" and "beta" represent the two technical components that describe a fund's (or stock's) performance relative to the market movement. Beta represented the correlation with the market, the part that can be explained by the market index movement, and alpha was the remainder, the part that was independent of the market; alpha was the outperformance. Investors were looking for that portion that couldn't be explained by the market, they were looking for strategies that performed well when the market movement was flat.

One of the most popular alternative investment strategies would become "market-neutral" equity. "Market neutral" is a term to describe a portfolio of equally weighted long and short positions, which is consequently "neutral" in dollar terms. In a market-neutral strategy, a $100 million portfolio would have $50 million of long positions and $50 million of short positions. The belief is that the balanced dollar weights protect the portfolio from adverse market movements, thus offering protection against a market correction.

As the hedge fund industry matured, market-neutral hedge funds would be one of the more popular types of investment strategies, growing from fewer than 50 funds in the early 1990s to more than several hundred in 2008. Assets under management in these funds would grow from less than $20 billion in the mid-1990s to $160 billion at their peak of popularity in 2007.

Market-neutral investing had been around for decades, literally. Alfred Jones, the pioneer of the hedge funds, credited for the creation of the industry's first alternative asset management firm in 1949, was a practitioner of market-neutral investing. Jones believed that price movements of an individual asset were largely a function of the market and a component of the asset itself. His investment philosophy was to buy assets he expected would rise and to hedge with assets expected to fall.

Despite the pioneering efforts of Jones' flagship hedge fund, there would be little demand for market-neutral investing before the 1990s. The baby boomer generation was clearly depicted as a period of economic growth, expansionary policies, industrialization, and over-whelming increases in the valuation of U.S. equity markets. Hedging, as a result, was not a priority to the baby boomers.

In wasn't until the late 1990s that alternative asset managers would grow in appeal and market-neutral hedge funds would sprout in demand. There would be many new entrants to the market-neutral investment management, from traditional value-based stock selectors to quantitative traders. This investment strategy was challenging, however, for value-oriented managers who picked a basket of stocks that they liked and shorted it against a basket that they didn't like.

Market-neutral investing had many more nuances than just main-taining neutrality on a dollar basis. There were many variables that had investors concerned for adverse exposure: beta neutral to dampen the sensitivity to market movements; currency neutral to reduce exchange-rate risk across international markets; gamma neutral to hedge against volatility. Technology, too, played a role in the proficiency of a market-neutral firm. For portfolios that contained hundreds of stocks to remain "neutral" to market risks required a firm with the ability to monitor risk exposure in real time and to devise optimized hedging strategies. Market-neutral strategies were ideally suited for empirically minded fund managers.

In 1998, when Cliff Asness and his team at Goldman Sachs Quan-titative Strategies departed to form their own hedge fund, Applied Quantitative Research (AQR) Capital, they successfully raised $1 bil-lion of assets on the first day of their inception. AQR Capital raised more money in a single day than any other hedge fund. Quantita-tive market-neutral funds were just beginning to raise the bar on the sophistication of market-neutral investment strategies, and investors were incredibly excited about this next generation of hedge fund, which would truly embody the marriage of science and economics.

## WINNERS AND LOSERS

AQR Capital was one of the most heavily anticipated hedge fund start-ups at the time of its launch. Cliff Asness, the principal founder, earned a Ph.D. at the University of Chicago, where he was a research assistant to Eugene Fama. In 1997, Asness' team of financial engineers at Goldman Sachs had generated a 150 percent return on market-neutral trading. Investors were excited because AQR Capital had both the track record and the pedigree of the next generation of hedge funds.

Quantitative market-neutral strategies would have appeal with traditional investors because their investment strategy was founded on economic principles. Unlike high-frequency black-box trading, such as statistical arbitrage, that searches for technical discrepancies that arise due to supply and demand imbalances, market-neutral strategies would be searching for longer-term anomalies that arise due to economic reasons. Market-neutral firms would not be concerned with market inefficiencies defined by momentum, moving averages, stochastic, and so on, but rather they would target price anomalies of the efficient market price, defined by the capital asset pricing model (CAPM).

In finance, the CAPM is a model to derive the theoretical rate of return of a stock. Jack Treynor, William Sharpe, John Linter, and Jan Mossin first introduced the model in the 1960s, and it has remained the formal approach for deriving a stock's efficient market price. The CAPM assumes the expected return of a stock is a function of the risk-free interest rate, the expected return of the market and the stock's correlation with the market (i.e. beta). In theory, an asset is priced fairly if its market price is in line with that produced by the model.

Stock prices deviate from those derived by the CAPM frequently. A "price anomaly" to the CAPM is a repetitive pattern of deviation that is attributed to differences in firm characteristics such as P/E ratio, book-to-market ratio, sales growth, earnings momentum, and currency exposure. Consequently, market-neutral strategies are based on intuitive economic theories on the firm characteristics that contribute to overvalued or undervalued stocks.

Academic research has recounted many different types of price anomalies of the CAPM approach. Momentum effects, such as the tendency for stocks with strong 12-month returns to outperform the market in the subsequent 12 months, have been highlighted in many studies. Reversal effects, in which stocks with successive low-earnings results have tended to outperform the market on a long-term horizon, have been attributed to investor biases that lead to inefficient pricing.

Size effects, too, have been published to highlight how a stock's expected return is more closely related to its market capitalization than the efficient model's price.

Eugene Fama and Kenneth French published one of the most prominent anomalies of the CAPM in the early 1990s. They showed that historical returns of the S&P 500 over the past century have highlighted consistent patterns in the relationships between stocks and their forward returns.[2] Stocks that are priced low relative to their earnings (i.e. low P/E ratios) outperform those that are priced high. An article, published in the *Journal of Finance*, described this effect as the "value premium" (see figure 5.2).

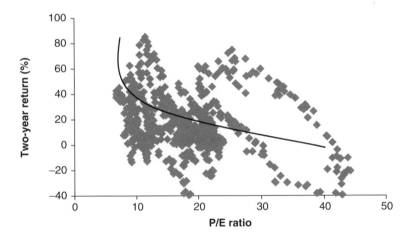

**FIGURE 5.2** Relative value strategies

The value premium describes the empirical research that "value" stocks tend to outperform "growth" stocks in the long term. In finance, a value stock is a firm with a strong balance sheet (i.e. very little debt) and high cash flow. A value stock is described, empirically, by a high book-to-market ratio, a high earnings-per-share, or a high cash flow-per-share ratio. Public utilities are the most frequent example of value stocks. The research by French and Fama showed that value firms were unfairly discounted relative to growth stocks. Investors, correspondingly, have fared better when they buy stocks at lower valuations, single-digit P/E ratios, and hold for the long term.

The value premium associated with low P/E ratios and higher long-term returns is a discrepancy of the CAPM. The rationale to explain this empirical relationship is that investors buy growth stocks that are too expensive, particularly in periods of economic prosperity (i.e. high P/E ratios of the market as a whole). Despite intuitive evidence of inflated valuations, investors often find ways of convincing themselves that this time is different. They buy into the flavor of the month, whether it's Priceline.doc or an emerging gold mine.

There has been considerable empirical research into the market behavior and the psychology of individual decision making. The area of research is known as "behavioral economics" and is concerned with understanding empirical discrepancies that arise from the behavior of investors around the release of information such as poor earnings results, dividend adjustments, and economic developments. The behavioral economists suggest that individuals tend to overweight recent events and underweight prior information, which leads to a bias in investors' judgment and periodic observations when the stock market "overreacts" to insignificant information.

In his book, *Theory of Investment Value*, Williams commented that stock prices have been based too much on current earnings power and too little on the long-term dividend-paying power. His findings suggested that stock-price movements are strongly correlated with the following year's earnings changes and highlight a clear pattern of overreaction. Empirical evidence over the past half a century confirms that dividends do not vary significantly enough to explain the corresponding volatility in the asset prices. Investors, presumably, place too much weight on the short-term results rather than the long-term fundamentals of the corporation to sustain dividend payouts.

In an article appearing in the *Journal of Finance*, Richard Thaler, a prominent academic in behavioral finance, showed evidence on a long-standing investor bias known as the "P/E ratio anomaly." This anomaly refers to the observation that stocks with extremely low P/E ratios earn larger risk-adjusted returns than high-P/E stocks.[3] The hypothesis is that companies with very low P/Es are "undervalued" because investors are thought to be overly pessimistic after a series of bad earnings, management restructuring, or similarly related uncertainties.

He formulated a strategy to exploit this bias. Stocks that experience excessive capital gains over a three-year period could be categorized as "winners," and stocks that experience extreme loses could be bucketed as "losers." By buying losers and selling winners, a portfolio could be constructed to capture the overreaction effects. The results were impressive: over the past half-century, their research suggested that

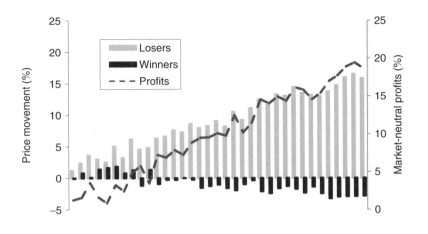

**FIGURE 5.3**   Winners and losers strategy

the loser portfolio outperformed the winner portfolio by an average of 8.1 percent annually (see figure 5.3).

This is the appeal of market-neutral investing. A portfolio constructed that's neutral to equity valuation, dividend yield, and financial leverage can yield positive returns regardless of the market environment. Market-neutral investors can still earn excess returns in the midst of stock market corrections, increases in long-term financing rates, and cyclical economic downturns.

Econometric research, such as the value premium, laid the foundation for market-neutral investing. By having a model that describes the "relative" value of stocks, market-neutral managers could construct portfolios of long positions in undervalued stocks with short positions in overvalued stocks, capturing the inefficiencies in their valuations. A value-versus-growth portfolio, for instance, could capture the expected excess returns while being "neutral" to the market's return as a whole.

The academic evidence by a broad group of economists, such as Thaler, Williams, French, and Fama has validated the market-neutral investment philosophy. What is particularly interesting to the black-box community is the validation of empirical metrics to describe the relative value of stocks. Rather than studying the business model or meeting with the company's CEO and CFO, an investment firm can rank firms based on their empirical characteristics: essentially identifying "high" quality stocks and "low" quality stocks, relative to one another.

## RISK FACTOR MODELS

Market-neutral strategies identify high-quality and low-quality stocks by comparison of "risk factor" analysis. Risk factors are variables that measure the risk of a stock relative to the market. They are metrics that allow investors to gage a particular type of risk across a range of stocks, such as debt, exposure to interest rates, or sensitivity to inflation. Risk factors are often traditional balance-sheet metrics, such as book-to-market ratio or P/E ratio, and they are also derived metrics to quantify a stock's sensitivity to another variable.

Black-box firms apply risk factor analysis to understand the relative value of stocks better and to model price anomalies. A risk factor model ranks stocks relative to their peers. Through their econometric research, quantitative managers determine which risk factors have the strongest statistical significance in pricing stocks, relative to one another (see table 5.1).

**Table 5.1**  Risk factors

| | |
|---|---|
| P/E RATIO | The ratio of the current market price to the earnings per share |
| BOOK-TO-MARKET RATIO | The ratio of the net asset value to the market capitalization |
| CASH FLOW-TO-PRICE RATIO | The ratio of cash revenue inflows per share to the current market price |
| EARNINGS MOMENTUM | The projected monthly growth of earnings per share |
| DIVIDEND YIELD | The rate of return of dividends based on share price |
| SENIOR DEBT RATIO | The amount of bonds (or other forms of debt) outstanding to the market capitalization |

There are many reasons risk factors vary across stocks and across sectors. Differences in accounting practices, capital structure, and source of debt will influence how a firm's net asset value is derived, and correspondingly how it compares to that of its peers. For instance, in pharmaceutical companies, the P/E ratios differ greatly across the stocks within the sectors as a reflection of the difference in expected growth rate of firms. Quantitative researchers will study the historical levels of these variables to determine whether there is any statistical significance to the future returns.

Risk factor analysis is particularly useful in understanding the differences across industries and within industries. Studies have shown that a better forecast for future returns can be obtained by breaking down explanatory variables into industry-specific terms. The difference between stocks' own characteristics and the average of the market can explain the reasons for an observed outperformance to its sector.

Earnings momentum, for instance, may not be comparable between entertainment firms and construction firms, for obvious reasons given the uniqueness of the industries. But looking at earnings momentum across a single sector may lend interesting insights into the best and worse stocks in that industry group. Market-neutral models, consequently, are often designed to be "sector neutral," betting on the winners and losers within an industry, in addition to being dollar neutral as a whole.

There are considerable incentives for picking the winners and losers within a sector. The average sector dispersion (the difference between the best and worst performers) varies from 2.0 percent per month to 8.0 percent per month. A successful market-neutral strategy can yield a considerable profit with little exposure to the overall market trend (see figure 5.4).

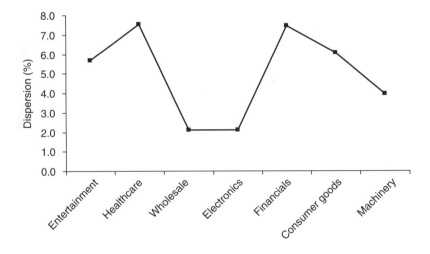

**FIGURE 5.4**  Average dispersion by sector

The quantitative research process was also well suited for understanding a portfolio's sensitivity to hypothetical scenarios in the market. Black-box firms could simulate their strategy's performance against movements in commodity prices, changes in interest rates, or currency depreciations. They could look at the historical impact of dividend reductions or corporate restructurings. Quantitative analysis was a successful approach to market-neutral investing because it was validating economic theories within a robust research framework.

Quantitative strategies also benefit from the luxury of backtests using the historical data. Although historical simulations do not predict future returns, they allow fund managers to understand better the model's risk–reward relationship and the sensitivity to various indicators. Through backtests, quantitative managers can assess their portfolio's sensitivity to a variety of risk factors, throughout different economic climates.

Market-neutral strategies generated a broad appeal to traditional investors because they are based on intuitive economic principles and they are easily articulated. Market-neutral firms were the true complement of science and economics, so they were successful at attracting institutional investors.

## THE LEVERAGE EFFECT

Market-neutral strategies are a type of "relative value" strategy, in which each investment opportunity is evaluated relative to another in terms of risk, liquidity, and return. Through the usage of hedging one stock to another, relative-value strategies become independent (or uncorrelated) to the direction of the market. They can make money in bull or bear market environments.

Despite the attractiveness of nondirectional strategies, it is often difficult for investors to understand the upside potential intuitively. If an investor were investing in an emerging market, such as Russia for instance, the investor would have some reference for the upside (and downside) potential based on historical volatilities and the prevailing sentiments of the economic climate. But how is an investor to formulate a view on the potential return of a market-neutral strategy?

The returns of market-neutral strategies depend on a different set of metrics than traditional investments. By hedging, market-neutral firms effectively reduce the exposure to the market volatility and directional movements. On an annualized basis, an investor purchasing an S&P 500 index fund could expect to make 30 percent return in a good year and lose 30 percent in a bad year. This is based on the historical volatility of the S&P 500 being in the range of 2 percent daily. A market-neutral strategy, conversely, is designed to minimize the portfolio's variance through the combination of long and short positions.

A linear combination of two stocks, such as buying Yahoo! and shorting eBay, will reduce the volatility by 50 percent. For instance, during 2008 the spread between the Yahoo! and eBay stocks averaged a narrow 10 percent price range, despite observing a directional trend of −70 percent throughout one of the most volatile years in the history of the U.S. markets (see figure 5.5).

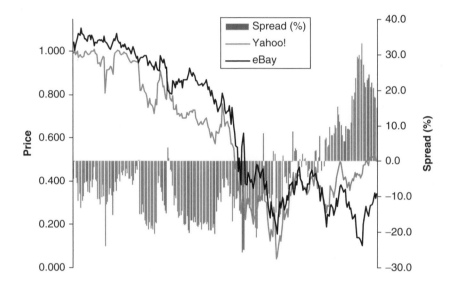

**FIGURE 5.5**   Yahoo! and eBay spread trade
Note: The price index has been normalized from a base value of 1.0

Market-neutral hedge funds attempt to financial-engineer strategies that minimize volatility through diversification and hedging strategies. Because they combine long/short positions between correlated stocks, they engineer their desired risk–reward characteristics and dampen the annualized volatility significantly.

Market-neutral strategies depend on the overall market volatility and the "dispersion" of returns within the index and sector. Dispersion, defined as the difference between the best and worst stocks within a group, is an important determinant for the profits of market-neutral strategies. If dispersion is large, there is a greater potential to outperform the market by picking the winners (and losers) within the sector.

A portfolio of only two correlated stocks might have a monthly dispersion in the 5–10 percent range. But as the number of stocks in the portfolio increases, the aggregate range of dispersion decreases to only a few percentage points per month. Consequently, an optimized portfolio of a thousand securities may have an annualized volatility of less than 10 percent.

Market-neutral firms, as a result, depend on leverage to magnify their returns. Investors desire low volatility monthly but at the same time they want double-digit annual returns. Market-neutral firms employ leverage to magnify the returns of their portfolios, where even the most proficient stock selectors may require 2× or 4× leverage to achieve double-digit returns.

A firm with $1 billion in assets under management may leverage its strategies to be $2 billion long and $2 billion short, considerably magnifying its presence in the marketplace. And with all its peers also depending on leverage, a $100 billion industry of market-neutral investment firms blossomed into an important source of liquidity to the marketplace.

## THE DISPERSION EFFECT

Market-neutral strategies are employed by hundreds of hedge funds and proprietary trading firms. The more prominent hedge funds such as AQR Capital, Black Mesa, SAC Capital, D.E. Shaw, Highbridge, Stark, Millennium, and Marshall Wace have grown into multibillion dollars of market-neutral strategies. Given that internal proprietary trading desks, such as those operated by Goldman Sachs, Morgan Stanley, UBS, Deutsche Bank, and so on, also have billions of assets allocated to market-neutral trading, ringfencing the total amount of industry assets is impractical.

An independent survey provider on hedge funds, estimated the peak of their assets at more than $120 billion in 2007. There is no industry watchdog, however, that can estimate the total value of the market exposure when leverage is considered. At the peak of its prominence, before the 2008 financial crisis, market-neutral investing could have easily represented more than $500 billion of leveraged positions in the market.

Even though their econometric models may be searching for long-term anomalies, the sheer size of these firms by assets under management means they generate a large footprint of trading volume. It's conceivable that market-neutral investors could represent anywhere from 5–10 percent of the world's daily trading activity.

The influence of market-neutral firms is subtle given that their strategies are nondirectional. Their trading activity has a different role in the marketplace: they dampen volatility. One of the more pronounced trends in the global equity markets was profiled in an issue of *The Barra Newsletter*, produced by MSCI Barra, the leader in risk management and portfolio analytics.[4] Barra highlighted that the global equity markets have been observing declines in the "cross-sectional" volatility or "dispersion."

Dispersion had been stable for a long period leading up to the Russian default crisis in 1998, where it had hovered between 7 percent and 9 percent for the monthly returns of U.S. equity markets. After 1998, global equity market dispersion rose to 13 percent and then peaked at 23 percent during the internet bubble (see figure 5.6).

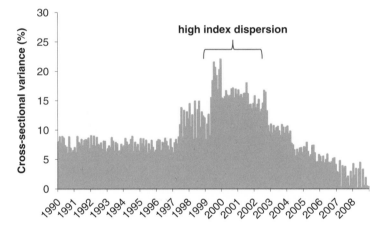

**FIGURE 5.6**   S&P monthly dispersion

Subsequently, the trend has been downward towards historical lows of less than 5 percent in 2006. Although economists are divided on the interpretations of the recent trends in equity dispersion, studies suggest the growth of relative-value strategies, such as market-neutral investing, has played a crucial role in dampening sector dispersion.

One study by academics at the University of Chicago postulates an interesting view on the role of market-neutral investors. They are "contrarian" investors betting against traditional investors. By ranking stock with risk factor models, market-neutral firms are disproportionately buyers in stocks that are undervalued and sellers in stocks that are overvalued. They are contrarian investors, who characteristically are buying "distressed" stocks that other investors feel are out-of-flavor, and are selling "glamour" stocks, in which investors have placed too much emphasis on recent performance.

In that light, market-neutral investors are a unique form of liquidity provider. They offer liquidity where other investors have lost interest. Consequently, their trading activities will dampen the dispersion between the market's winners and losers. The pronounced declines in equity dispersion over the past decade are a testament to their influence.

Economists may be divided on the interpretations of the recent trends in equity dispersion, but they are in agreement in one respect: the opportunities for profiting on market-neutral strategies have dwindled as more hedge funds are chasing the same winners and losers.

# CHAPTER 6

# The Arms Race

### Why a Company's Trading Volume Is More Closely Watched than Its Earnings

O ne of the most widely viewed financial pages is the list of "most active" stocks on the day. This is a summary list of the most actively traded stocks by market volume. It can usually be found alongside tables showing the "biggest gains" and "biggest losses." Even the most novice of retail investors is familiar with the value of these brief market summaries, because the data provide a quick snapshot of the activity on the day, and allow an investor to observe whether there are any outliers from the normal market movements.

The most active stocks are predominately large-capitalization stocks. The top-10 most active U.S.-listed stocks would most certainly include Microsoft, General Electric, Procter & Gamble, and Wal-Mart regularly, if not every day. An outlier would be seeing a lesser-known firm breaching the top 10. An investor would know immediately that there must have been an event to trigger the elevated trading volume. A drug company may have received a long-awaited regulator approval for a new vaccine; a mining firm may have uncovered a repository of gold; an accounting firm may be linked to rumors of a scandal. Information drives the relative level of trading activity in the stock market.

The most active lists, however, say little about how the volume arrived in the market. Did it occur during the market open? Was trading elevated around the market close? Was there a large block in the middle of the day? Is the distribution of volume linear or is it elevated around the arrival of new information?

In London, the most active period of the trading session is the market's closing auction, in which on average 5.5 percent of the volume occurs in the final transaction of the session. The opening auction on the LSE barely commands 1 percent of the day's activity. On an average day, stocks on the LSE open light and then trading activity increases

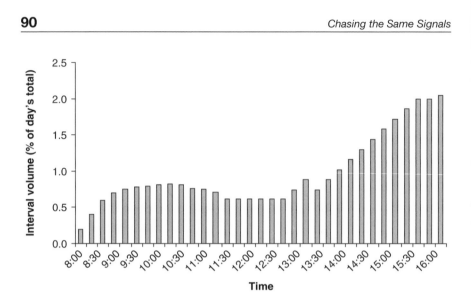

**FIGURE 6.1a**    LSE—distribution of volume

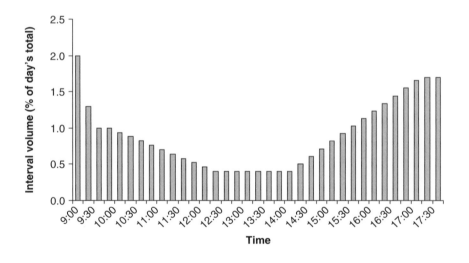

**FIGURE 6.1b**    Borsa Italiana—distribution of volume

throughout the afternoon, with the peak in the closing auction (see figure 6.1a).

In Italy, conversely, the distribution of volume is a different story. The opening auction and closing auctions are both moderately active with 4.5 percent of the day's activity. There is no skew toward one side of the trading session, as in London. Stock activity in Italy, however, after opening strong in the morning auction usually tapers off toward the middle of the day, and then grows in strength an hour before the closing auction. A chart of the volume distribution resembles a "smile curve," with peaks in the open and close and a dip in the middle (see figure 6.1b). This is a normal day in Italy.

An investor may wonder why London and Italy have very distinct patterns in their volume distributions. Is this because information arrives at different times in different countries or because the local traders have a different execution strategy? Do portfolio managers make investment decisions at different times of the day? Does the regulatory environment influence the periods of higher liquidity? Does the distribution of volume convey any information to investors?

The distribution of volume, although not a widely quoted feature of a stock, is arguably one of the most audited metrics in the financial industry. Hundreds of millions of research dollars are invested each year by Wall Street firms to understand better the sensitivity of volume, across stocks and across different periods of the day.

What influences the volume of a stock? Why does one stock trade more at the open and less at the close? What signals are more likely than others to trigger a volume spike? These are the questions Wall Street's quantitative research analysts are asking.

Their emphasis on volume is very straightforward: execution is essential for their business. Market-neutral and statistical arbitrage strategies all share a common plight: frictional effects, such as brokerage commissions, erode the profits of a successful quantitative strategy. As the global markets have observed declines in volatility, serial-correlation and cross-sectional variation, there has been a corresponding decay in the margins of black-box strategies. Even if the models employed have predictive power, their margin for error has become smaller.

Ever since the birth of the electronic marketplace, more eyes are watching a stock's distribution of volume than its earnings announcements. These investors aren't waiting for the end-of-day lists of most active stocks, but rather they are watching the relative activity at every moment throughout the day. Any deviation from the normal distribution represents a potential outliner event. An increase of volume during a 10-minute interval is just as likely to cause a rally in the stock's price as an announcement from the firm's CEO.

Sourcing liquidity has evolved from an industry of block transactions, negotiated between financial intermediaries, toward an automated marketplace where transactions occur between comput-erized investors, each with unique risk preferences and investment objectives. Volume has become the single common denominator that every black-box trading strategy is chasing.

## THE SUPPLIERS AND DEMANDERS OF LIQUIDITY

In July 2009, Sinopec Corp., also known as the China Petroleum & Chemical Corporation, became the first Chinese corporation to be ranked in the top 10 of the Fortune 500. Since the rankings were based on 2008 revenues, Sinopec's milestone was the direct result of historical high oil prices and the financial turmoil, which displaced the largest U.S. banking institutions from the top 10. It was a historic moment, nevertheless.

Sinopec's business includes oil and gas exploration, refining, chem-ical fibers, fertilizers, storage, natural gas, and as an import/export agency business, crude oil. Its stock is listed on the Shanghai Stock Exchange (SSE), the Hong Kong Stock Exchange (HKEx), and the NYSE.

Sinopec rose in prominence throughout China's emergence on the world financial stage. As the Chinese economy was marching along at double-digit growth, and oil prices climbed from $30 to north of $150 at its peak, the market capitalization of Sinopec rose by sevenfold, into one of the largest companies in the world. But, for many years before oil's appreciation, Sinopec was nowhere near a Fortune 500 candidate, and not a regular headline in the financial news.

On January 23, 2002 came a case in point: nothing happened. It was a typical trading day for Sinopec in those days. There was no news or announcements. Record oil prices were not in the headlines. Sinopec's share price opened at HK$1.06 and closed one cent lower at HK$1.05. There was no reason to mention Sinopec on the evening news.

The most recent company report had been released on January 16, regarding Li Yizhong, the prevailing president of Sinopec, disclosing a joint venture with British Petroleum to cooperate on 500 filling stations in Zhejiang province. This information, however, had been speculated for months and had long been reflected in Sinopec's share price. The HKEx market as a whole had very light trading volumes on January 23. It was only a couple weeks before the Lunar New Year and many Chinese individuals were (and are) superstitious about doing risky business transactions before their annual festival holiday, so market volumes suffer a seasonality effect.

Although nothing happened on January 23, something happened. At 11.04 a.m., over an hour into the market open, a block of shares transacted. The block represented 63 percent of the volume on the day. It was more shares than normally transact in an average day in Sinopec; the block represented twice the average trading volume for the previous 30 days (see figure 6.2).

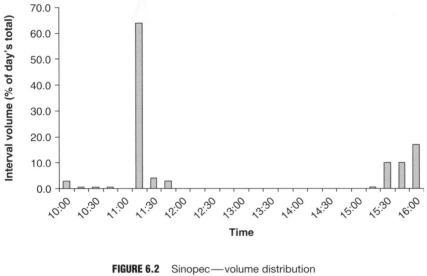

**FIGURE 6.2**   Sinopec—volume distribution
*Source:* Bloomberg

An investor needed liquidity is what happened that morning. A buyer in Sinopec was willing to buy all the shares at the prevailing best offer prices of 1.07 and 1.08 in a single instance. The buyer effectively paid a 1 percent premium (HK0.02 cents) above the most recent transaction to purchase shares immediately. Sinopec's share price spiked momentarily, then the market went quiet, with only a few transactions before the market close. The last transactions on the day were initiated by sellers, who were hitting the market's best bids at HK$1.05.

Despite all the fancy trading strategies that have emerged in the past decade, the marketplace can still be broken down into two categories of investors: liquidity suppliers and liquidity demanders. The "liquidity demander" is the individual that initiates the transaction. In industry lingo, he or she is the investor (or trader) who "hits" a bid or "lifts" an offer. The term "demand" is affiliated with the investors' demand for a counterparty to transact with.

The "liquidity supplier" is the counterparty investor whose shares were hit or lifted in the market's queue. A liquidity supplier is an investor who is willing to transact only at his or her specific price, and is content to wait patiently in the queue until another investor meets his or her price. The demander, on the other hand, has an urgency to complete the transaction. These are the investors willing to pay a premium (i.e. pay the bid–offer spread), rather than wait in the queue and potentially have the market drift away from them. The demander has an aversion to taking on market exposure and is reluctant to wait.

What transpired at 11.04 a.m. on January 23 is known as a "window of liquidity." For whatever catalyst at that time, the buyer demanded to complete his or her order and was willing to pay a premium. He or she may have had a long-term view on the stock, over and above the costs of the spread; he or she may have correspondingly sold a block of PetroChina, a similar China-listed company, and was underweight in the oil and gas sector; he or she might have been a speculator, hoping to ignite a rally in the share price.

The liquidity supplier, on the other hand, could have had any number of objectives for waiting in the offer queue. He or she could be a long-term investor who was only willing to sell at HK$1.07 or higher. He or she could be local dealer, who was willing to buy stock at HK$1.05 and sell at HK$1.07, for a tiny profit. In either case, he or she did not have an immediate urgency to initiate a transaction.

This is the common interaction between all investors: making a trade-off of costs versus risk. In their book *Optimal Trading Strategies*, Robert Kissell and Morton Glantz described this as the "trader's dilemma." If a trader executes too aggressively, he or she incurs high market impact costs; if he or she executes too passively, he or she is exposed to significant timing risk, which could result in even greater costs because of adverse price movements. The trader is responsible for determining the trade-off between these conflicting objectives.[1]

Costs, however, are a very subjective topic. Some are fixed, such as brokerage fees and settlement costs, while others are not well defined, such as market impact and opportunity costs. What is known is that costs vary greatly from region to region, and they are one of the biggest factors governing the behavior between suppliers and demanders. Consequently, the costs of trading have a direct effect on the liquidity of the marketplace.

# THE SIGNIFICANCE OF MARKET STRUCTURE

The reason the LSE and the Borsa Italiana differ in their volume distribution has little to do with the fundamental appeal of the stocks listed on these markets. These countries are both attractive in light of a growing pan-European economy. They are also subject to similar risks, because the impact of recession in one country would have a knock-on effect in another. This interdependent relationship is reflected in the strong correlation between the LSE's FTSE-100 and Italy's S&P/MIL-30 indexes, which has increased every year since the launch of the euro.

The relationship between the intraday liquidity distributions of the two countries is a different story. How investors access liquidity in these markets is distinct and largely influenced by the uniqueness of the market structure, rather than the fundamentals of their economies. The domain of "market structure" broadly characterizes the stock market in terms of market mechanisms, regulatory environment, and makeup of the financial community. A comprehensive analysis of market structure from region to region would encompass several fields of economics, each having strong views on the factors that influence market liquidity. For understanding the distribution of volume, a perspective on the market mechanisms of how stocks are traded is most insightful on why trading activity arrives in the morning in Italy, but in the afternoons in London.

The LSE is strongly influenced by activities in the U.S markets, given that London is the established financial center for Europe. Volume on the LSE is skewed toward the late afternoon when the U.S markets open, which is about 2.30 p.m. GMT. In Italy, although the market is also influenced by the U.S. openings, the morning auction on the Borsa Italiana attracts heavy volumes around their index futures and single-options expiry process, which leads to hedging transactions in the morning auction. Derivation transactions create change in beneficial ownership, which involves unique tax obligations, and result in heavy trading activity.

Despite the fact the investment community may view Europe as an integrated marketplace, whose economies are all influenced by the same fundamental risks, how a trader executes in each country is very different because of the market structure. The pan-Europe marketplace has staggered opening market times, unique rules for minimum price steps, auctions at both the open and close, auctions middle of the day, unique tax rules, distinct regulations on futures and options trading, and so on. The uniqueness of the market structure plays a significant role in how and when liquidity arrives in the market.

The resultant volume distribution is the culmination of these unique aspects of the local market structure because each mechanism influences the individuals willing to supply liquidity.[2] The HKEx, where most of Sinopec's volume is traded, is a classic example of how the market structure influences the distribution of volume. The HKEx is one of the world's most highly transparent exchanges in terms of the real-time information disseminated to its members. Brokers' names are disseminated to the other brokers alongside their orders in the queue. A broker with orders in the bid queue and the offer queue would have his or her name visible to his or her competitors. Although there are several hundred local brokerage houses, any one player trading in large blocks would be identified to the financial community.

The HKEx has additional nuances, which are unique to any major global marketplace: the exchange's order book throttles brokers at three orders per second, to constrain the rate of trading. This constraint, originating from the HKEx's migration to an electronic platform in 1995, was imposed to maintain a level playing field between local brokers and the foreign firms. Since a local dealer was thought capable of typing only one order every three seconds into the exchange terminal, the HKEx decided to constrain electronic gateways to the same threshold, ensuring that local dealers were not at a disadvantage to the technology-heavy global investment banks.

Liquidity providers must also consider local taxes. The Hong Kong Monetary Authority (HKMA), in light of capital gains taxes, imposes stamp taxes of 12.5 basis points per transaction. Any speculator wishing to provide short-term liquidity will pay 0.25 percent in round-trip taxes, regardless of whether he or she earned a profit or a loss.

The resulting effect on liquidity is that there are no investors willing to transact for tiny margins. It takes at least a round-trip return of 0.50 percent to overcome the frictional effects of trading, inclusive of brokerage, settlement, and local taxes. This is why bid–offer spreads in Sinopec, before oil was trading above $100, averaged 60 basis points. Liquidity providers have high costs to overcome before making a short-term profit.

Hong Kong, Italy, and London are three very different cases of market structure, each with different patterns of volume distribution. How an investor accesses the liquidity in different regions must conform with the local market structure. The fact that Wall Street firms spend millions of research dollars each year on analyzing the volume distribution from one country to the next is a function of the incentives for having a better forecast than one's competitor. Minimizing transaction costs, through optimization of execution, has become one of the most differentiated aspects of a fund's performance. In the modern financial marketplace, how you trade is equally as important as what you trade.

## THE SIGNIFICANCE OF TRANSACTION COSTS

Fund performance is not only a function of a successful investment strategy, but also a function of its ability to source liquidity efficiently. The mutual fund industry was the first to experience the role of execution: costs are a huge determinant of a fund's performance.

In the 1990s, there was a variety of academic research into one of the less glamorous aspects of asset management: transaction costs. Transaction costs are the friction effects incurred when implementing a fund's investment strategy. These are the costs of brokerage commissions, settlement and clearing fees, taxes, market impact, and opportunity costs. Although they are not as glamorous as research conferences or meetings with CFOs, academic research has highlighted that transaction costs contribute to a fund's performance just as much as successful stock selection.

A study by the Wharton School of Finance, across a random sample of 132 mutual funds, quantified that there is an inverse relationship between a fund's transaction costs and its performance. In its sample period, funds that were in the highest quintile of expense ratios had average returns of 9.76 percent, while funds with the lowest costs had achieved returns of 14.52 percent. The best funds had the lowest transaction costs (see figure 6.3).

Academic research has also shown that fixed costs are only one aspect of transactions. Although larger asset managers will benefit from lower brokerage commissions because of their negotiating power, their size has only limited benefits in reducing their cost structure. As commissions decline, the role of fixed costs becomes less pronounced in market-related costs. The Wharton study showed that average brokerage commissions for the largest U.S. mutual fund managers were in the range of 30 basis points, while transaction costs due to the bid–offer spread were 47 basis points.[3] More than 60 percent of a fund's total costs were market related.

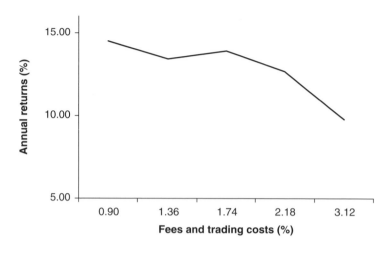

**FIGURE 6.3**  Fund performance versus transaction costs

The more startling findings in the academic research were the variance of market-related trading costs across mutual funds. The different in market-related costs between the best-performing funds and the worst was 59 basis points. The worst-performing funds were paying twice as much in trading costs as brokerage costs. The difference in fund performance was largely led by quality of their execution.

The cost of "paying the spread", that is, being a liquidity demander, is much more than a few basis points here and there; it could put a fund out of business over time. Asset managers must have a process to model and manage transaction costs over time, and optimize the risk–reward relationship. The trader's dilemma of navigating the risk–reward frontier has become a science in itself.

The most essential ingredient in the management of frictional effects is an understanding of volume distribution. Kissell and Glantz provide an academic framework for modeling the costs of trading in their book, *Optimal Trading Strategies*. Frequently investors have orders that are much larger than the market can absorb at one moment. If an investor has an accurate forecast on volume, he or she can distribute his or her orders over time, so as to minimize the market impact and to avoid paying a premium. The cornerstone of market impact analysis is an empirical model for volume distribution.

In the modern electronic marketplace, the effort to minimize transaction costs optimally has become increasingly more academic and more sophisticated. It has led to one of the largest proliferations of black-box technology in the financial industry: algorithmic trading. What has transpired in the past decade can only be characterized as an arms race of trading technology.

## THE ERA OF ALGOS

The business of execution changed dramatically with the advent of electronic trading technology in the late 1990s. Execution transformed from a process of manually sourcing liquidity between counterparts, to a process of quantitatively modeling impact and sourcing liquidity across multiple liquidity venues. State-of-the-art technology became essential for a firm to navigate the market structure of local market mechanisms and to trade at higher frequencies.

Trading technology was necessary for a firm to gain priority in the exchange's order books, ahead of its competitors. The tactic is known as "queueing" strategy, in which a firm positions its orders to gain priority over its peers. This tactic increases the chances of being filled at the desired price, and minimizes the need to incur costs by paying the bid–offer spread. If you're behind others, you're constantly chasing the market; but if you are the first in the queue, you stand a better chance of trading at the prevailing market price. Trading technology is essential to gain priority.

Smart order routing technology (SORT) is the first layer of the automated execution technology. These are tactical algorithms that automate mechanical aspects of trading. For instance, a trader could use these algorithms to automate sending a block of shares to the market immediately at the opening bell, thus offering the best chance at gaining priority.

SORT, however, is merely a set of tools to improve the efficiency of traders. Investment managers are also in need of products to optimize their order execution. They need intelligent algorithms to minimize their transaction costs.

Algorithmic trading engines (or algos) are the higher layer of execution technology. These are financially engineered strategies to minimize an order's execution to an industry benchmark, such as the market's vwap or closing price. Sending an order to an algo, in that sense, is no different than giving it to a broker verbally with similar instructions; however, the algorithm has been financially engineered to minimize the transaction costs, using the latest of academic theories and state-of-the-art technology.

Traditional asset managers have been the largest sponsor of algos for two reasons: these systems are financially engineered to minimize transaction costs and they are offered at a lower commission rate to a manual trader. By using algos, an asset manager can reduce both the fixed costs and market-related costs of execution.

The industry rapidly adopted the usage of algos after the U.S market's migration to decimals. The TowerGroup, an independent research firm, proclaimed 2004 to be the "Year of the Algorithm," because during that year, electronic trading by U.S asset managers grew to more than 20 percent of their total execution business.

Subsequently, algorithmic trading has become one of the largest methods of accessing liquidity in the major global markets. The proliferation of algorithmic trading is understated by the asset managers' adoption of electronic trading alone because algorithm usage is amplified by the internal usage at brokerage firms. In recent years, brokers have become increasingly dependent on algos to handle their institutional client orders. Due to the economics of the industry, there have been greater demands on brokers to increase their scale and quality of execution. Many of the global investment banks have been able to double their client business with only a marginal increase in trading staff. If they receive a $20 million order in Cisco Systems, they might put $12 million into an algorithm and then execute $8 million manually based on their view on the market.

This is why IT spending by an average Wall Street firm has grown to more than $1 billion a year during the arms race of technology. Investment banks are using SORT and algos to handle upward of 30 percent of their client orders. Algos are a significant source of liquidity in today's marketplace, representing $30 billion–$40 billion of daily volume. Their influence on the marketplace is a rapid increase in speed of the markets and a rapid growth of small orders.

## THE FRAGMENTATION OF LIQUIDITY

Algorithmic trading has been one of the most influential elements in the market microstructure. The process of translating investors' supply and demand habits into price and volume characteristics is no longer dictated by traders timing the markets, but rather is driven by sophisticated algorithms searching for liquidity. As a byproduct, one of the most prominent market trends has been the fragmentation of liquidity. Each day, there are fewer and fewer block trades.

In almost every major global marketplace, there has been a massive decline in the average trade size in the past five years. From 2004 to 2008, the average size of a transaction on the NYSE has decreased from more than $30,000 to less than $5,000. The LSE, similarly, has observed its average trade size to decline from $25,000 to less than $3,000.

The trends in average trade size might not be entirely attributable to the growth of algorithmic trading, but algos are the overwhelming influence. As brokers have used algorithms to manage their client orders, the markets have observed a higher number of individual transactions with lower quantities. A $10 million order from an institutional client is likely to be executed in a succession of hundreds of small orders.

In Korea, a market where electronic trading by DMA is prohibited, the declining trend has been the same. The average trade size on the Korean Stock Exchange declined from $7,100 to $1,200 from 2004 to 2008 (see figure 6.4). This is a market where there are no ECNs, no DMA, and hedge funds must access the market through structured products. Brokers' internal usage of algorithms is the most likely culprit for the trend.

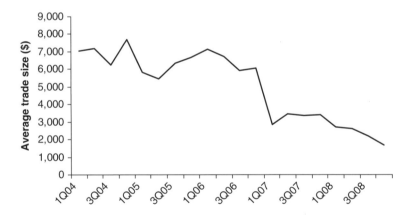

**FIGURE 6.4**    Trends in average trade size—Korea Stock Exchange
*Source:* World Federation of Exchanges

Algorithmic trading has become the modus operandi of all the major international brokerage houses, and the result has been a rapid migration from block transactions to small orders. How markets react to irregularities in volume is more pronounced than surprise earnings reports.

## _ _JNG TAIL OF MARKET IMPACT

On July 16, 2009, something happened. Investors in Oriental Overseas Limited, a shipping firm owned by Tung Che Hwa, former chief executive of Hong Kong Special Administrative Region, were handed a case of whiplash. The share price of Oriental dropped a dramatic 32 percent during the closing moments of the market's trading session. There was no news on the stock; nor any announcements or negative earnings reports; and the index was flat.

This event did make the headlines news. Reports commented on rumors of market manipulation. Anonymous sources in the financial community laid blame on the HKEx's closing auction, which had been suspended earlier in the year. The *Standard*, Hong Kong's local newspaper, reported an "erroneous program trade" in the postmortem.[4]

Oriental Overseas' 32 percent decline was the top of the "biggest losers" table. But the decline was shortlived. Oriental's share price rebounded at the open of the next trading session to its previous price level. For an evening, HK$7 billion of market capitalization was wiped from this prominent family-controlled shipping firm (see figure 6.5).

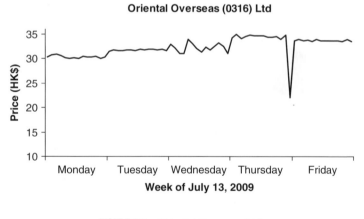

**Oriental Overseas (0316) Ltd**

**FIGURE 6.5**   Oriental Overseas Ltd.
*Source:* Bloomberg

Unfortunately for investors, there was no table on July 16 for "biggest declines in volume." This may have been more insightful into the dramatic collapse in share price. Average volume in Oriental at the market close was only a fraction of its average over the previous

30 days. The market impact was the inability of an algorithm to react to adversity.

Algorithms are designed to minimize market impact but they largely depend on forecasting liquidity. When liquidity is weak, algorithms may respond unpredictably to the adversity. Price impacts can be rapid and severe.

Compounding the problem is the diversity of market structure. Most banks design their models on U.S. market structure, and then port across to global markets. Many algorithms are poorly designed for emerging markets where the mechanisms are vastly unique. There are more trades in Google during a five-minute window than during an entire day for Alibaba. What is optimal in one market may be a loose cannon in another.

On an aggregate level, statistical arbitrage and market-neutral strategies have had a dampening effect on market's volatility and dispersion. But, given the proliferation of technology in the execution industry, on a per-trade basis, the tail of outlier events has become more pronounced in recent years. A 5 percent gain on the day used to be a big move, now it rarely makes the top-10 list. Only time will tell whether double-digit snapback becomes a regular occurrence for investors in global equity markets.

Investors may continue to read the day's "most active" lists, but they'll find fewer insights on the market's prevailing volatility. In the modern marketplace, a weak volume distribution is more severe than a poor quarterly earnings report.

# CHAPTER 7

# The Game of High Frequency

## *Why Nobody Has Heard of the Most Active Investors*

I n 2003, economist Harald Hau made an interesting observation on stocks that were traded on the Paris Bourse. Hau noticed that the volatility of stocks increased when their price increased. From an economics perspective, this was counterintuitive. A stock's volatility is assumed to be a reflection of the inherent fundamental risks in the company. Management restructuring, problems with the firm's products, and declines in consumer confidence were the common drivers of increasing a stock's volatility, because investors were less certain about the firm's future earnings potential. A rising share price, in light of fundamental changes in the company, would intuitively be a reflection of increased investor confidence; so why the increase in volatility in the absence of a change in fundamentals?

Economists in many parts of the world have debated the influences on market volatility. Why does Germany have a lower volatility than Greece? The political climate, breadth of investment strategies, quality of firms, local tax environment, and regulatory framework are all relevant factors that economists discuss as influential to the efficiency of the marketplace. But, in light of vastly different comparisons, why do similar companies have different volatility in different countries? Foreign firms listed on dual exchanges, such as many represented by American depository receipts (ADRs), often have lower volatility in the U.S. market than in their domestic country.

One factor that economists have suspected as an influence to volatility is transaction costs. Higher transaction costs are believed to discourage investors and reduce the diversity of investment strategies in the market. Costs, as a result, can play an influential role in the stock market's volatility. But economists have had few ways of deriving empirical research on this thesis.

Volatility is a particularly difficult phenomenon to research because it's greatly influenced by the economic cycle. The global markets observed years of declining volatility in the mid-2000s but then investors were treated to historical highs when the subprime crisis emerged. The difficulty for economists in researching volatility is isolating a factor across different economic periods.

The Paris Bourse provided a near-perfect natural experiment to analyze the role of transaction costs because it was a unique case in which one factor could be isolated to particular stocks, rather than the market as a whole. In the Paris Bourse, the size of the bid–offer spread is a fixed amount defined by the exchange. The Paris exchange governs the minimum price difference between buy orders and sell orders. This is known as its "tick size" rule.

The tick size is the minimum price difference between prices on a stock exchange. It is one of the most unique features of market structure across the major global markets. There are a few common rules for how an exchange defines its tick size, but on a global perspective there is no international standard. Some exchange uses a constant tick size across all products, while others use variable rates based on the price level of the stock.

For most of the past century, the tick size in the U.S. markets was one-eighth of a cent. In the 1990s, for the sake of efficiency, the tick size was reduced to one-sixteenth and then subsequently 0.01 cent when decimals were introduced in 2001/02. Most global markets, unlike the U.S. markets, have variable tick sizes, based on market rules that are familiar to their local investors. Tokyo stocks, for instance, may have a tick size of ¥1,000 for stocks priced above ¥1 million and a tick size of ¥100 for stocks priced below ¥10,000.

The Paris Bourse has a similar variable structure to Japan's, in which the tick size varies by price. The tick size is greater for stocks that are priced higher. There may be many different reasons they employ a variable tick structure, rather than a fixed increment, but likely it's because of the efficiency of the marketplace. Too small a tick size may create operational and settlement problems for brokers, clients, and the exchange systems.

The Paris Bourse provided a good natural experiment because volatility could be measured across stocks as they moved from one price band to the next. Stocks would be subject to higher tick size as they increased in share price. If their share price was below FF500, their tick size would be FF0.1; if their price rose above FF500, the tick size would increase to FF1.0; and vice versa. The tick size inflates by 20 percent when stocks crossed above the FF500 threshold. Given this structure, Harald Hau could perform a controlled experiment, studying the volatility of the same stocks across a variable tick regime, and across different economic climates.

Hau's empirical findings supported what many economics suspected. Higher transaction costs lead to greater market volatility.[1] In his study period, when stocks rose in value and across the FF500 threshold, they exhibit an increase in their volatility of 16 percent. Their volatility was influenced by the subtle rule of transaction costs, rather than a change in the fundamentals. Hau and other economists consider the frictional effects of the market structure a disadvantage to the investment community. Higher costs discourage short-term speculation, which correspondingly reduces the supply of liquidity.

Economists at least agree on the role that regulations and market structure have on market volumes. A variety of empirical evidence validates that market liquidity is inversely proportional to the costs of trading. Markets with the lowest frictional effects, such as the U.S. markets, attract foreign investors and cultivate a diverse variety of investment strategies. The interaction of these different investment strategies has a dampening effect on market volatility. The market structure thus plays an influential role on the characteristics of the market.

Transaction costs vary greatly across the global markets. Tax structure, brokerage commissions, exchange settlement and clearing fees, infrastructure, and operations all contribute to the realized costs of transacting in a particular market. The frictional effects alone are a large influence on trading volume.

With the evidence from the Paris Bourse and other economic studies, why don't exchanges reduce their cost structure? Wouldn't the entire financial community benefit from a greater supply of liquidity? These questions are part of one of the longest-standing debates in financial regulations. What is the appropriate treatment of speculators?

Economists and policymakers have long argued that speculative activity creates a destabilizing effect on the economy. John Maynard Keyes argued in his *General Theory of Employment, Interest and Money* for the introduction of a government transaction tax to mitigate the predominance of market speculators. He felt that speculative activities increased volatility and hindered long-term investors. Milton Friedman, however, had a contrary view on speculative activity: in his *Essays in Positive Economics* he suggested that speculators had a stabilizing role in the marketplace.

Economists agree on the difficulty of curtailing volatility through policy measures. Since there are so many factors that influence volatility, it's unrealistic for regulators to constrain all the potentially adverse behavior of the market participants. Investors cannot simply be constrained from panic selling during an economic crisis, for instance.

A small group of black-box firms, which are only a few years old, are now the latest chapter in the debate of market volatility. High-frequency trading firms have become the most active investors in the world. They have their hands in one out of every three trades in the U.S. markets. And nobody has heard of them.

## THE MOST ACTIVE INVESTORS

In the months after the subprime crisis, the global equity markets remained resilient in trading volume despite historical levels of fear among investors, worried about entering a 1930s-like era of depression. In most major global markets, turnover levels in 2009 were greater than in 2008. In part, market volumes remained resilient because investors, both institutional and retail, were fleeing the markets, but also, behind the scenes an emerging, niche industry was the driving force in buoying the global market turnover levels. These niche firms are so vague and ambiguous to the public that the best description put forth to characterize their brand of investment strategy is broadly: "high-frequency" trading.

A *Wall Street Journal* profile in August 2009 on one of these niche firms, Global Electronic Trading Co. (Getco), captured the public sentiments in the opening statement: "one of the biggest players in high-frequency trading is one of the least known."[2] Getco transacts in billions of shares each day, representing as much as 10 percent of the U.S. market volume; but few people have heard of it.

Getco, along with other less well-known firms—Knight Capital, Wedbush Morgan, Susquehanna—make up a small group of players involved in the game of high-frequency trading. Their label "high-frequency" is fitting because they are trading upward of a thousand orders per second.

Unlike other types of quantitative firms, high-frequency traders are not trying to capitalize on empirical price discrepancies, nor are they targeting arbitrage relationships. They do not depend on historical analysis of serial correlation, moving averages, or dispersion signals that statistical arbitrage and market-neutral firms are chasing. Many of these firms are not even registered hedge funds or broker–dealers, but rather unregulated, privately owned firms. They are a new breed of financial firm, focused on the one particular variable in the market: the bid–offer spread.

Their investment strategy is better described as "automated market making" (or AMM) given that their investment objective is to be continuously buying and selling securities during the market sessions, and they prefer to carry few or no positions after the market's close. They provide a continuous stream of liquidity to the marketplace and in return earn tiny profits on thousands of transactions.

The traditional understanding of a "market maker" is a firm (or individual) responsible for maintaining an orderly market between buyers and sellers. A registered market maker is obliged to provide a buy price and a sell price throughout the trading session with the incentive of making a profit on the bid–offer spread. Most importantly, it is an intermediary responsible for stabilizing imbalances between supply and demand, putting its capital at risk to maintain transactions when liquidity is scarce.[3]

NYSE specialists represent the most conventional understanding of the market maker. They are the official designated market makers, empowered by the exchange to maintain the efficiency of the order book. The NYSE is a unique case of market structure on a global perspective.[4] Most of the global exchanges, such as the Swiss Exchange, Paris Bourse, or TSE, are order-driven markets in which orders transact within the exchanges' centralized order book based on price-time priority.

Market making on order-driven markets exists through traditional "broker–dealers," such as global investment banks or boutique retail stock brokerages. Broker–dealers provide their clients with bid and offer prices for an immediate execution on orders. Investment banks are making markets for the institutional clients, usually for large block orders that would incur market impact if worked on the exchange. Retail brokers are making markets for individual investors, who prefer to let the broker manage the execution. In either case, the broker–dealer earns a profit from the price given to its client and the price of unwinding the position on the market.

Independent proprietary trading firms (or individuals) may also engage in market making. Japan's infamous DoCoMo Man was best described as a market maker, who made a livelihood by intraday trading in NTT DoCoMo. Although a special case given the unique nuances of Japan's market mechanisms, DoCoMo Man was an accurate representative of providing short-term liquidity and earning a profit margin in between the transactions of institutional clients.

The emergence of systematic firms in the game of AMM has been an iterative process, growing in prominence as the electronic marketplace has evolved. As early as the SEC's introduction of new order-handling rules in 1996, quantitative firms began to challenge traditional market makers in offering prices to the marketplace. The SEC's adoption of the "Limit Order Display Rule" enforced market makers and specialists to display the best available prices on ECNs publicly, which opened the door for the quantitative firms to broadcast their prices alongside the institutional market makers.

Technology enabled high-frequency firms to gain an edge. The SEC's adoption of Reg ATS in 1998 provided a framework to institutionalize the regulatory oversight into market prices, surveillance, and system stability. Reg ATS affected the entire financial community: it encouraged investment into ECNs, SORT systems, algos, and data vendors, and it benefited the efficiency of the marketplace. The arms race of technology allowed firms to increase their frequency of trading from seconds to milliseconds.

The most significant catalyst for automated market makers was the SEC's introduction of the Regulation of National Market Systems (Reg NMS) in June 2005. Among a variety of reforms to improve the competitiveness of the U.S. markets was the "Order Protection Rule." This rule enforced that all transactions must occur within the national best bid and offer (NBBO) price range. The rule ensures investors are not disadvantaged by transactions at worse prices than available on other venues; it also ensures that systematic market makers' orders, if better than the NBBO, would have priority.

The introduction of Reg NMS made the U.S. markets advantageous for high-frequency traders because it ensured that orders, from both institutional and retail investors, would need to transact at the best available market prices. By offering prices at the NBBO or better, AMMs could compete with traditional market makers. The game of high frequency became a contest of offering the lowest "spread" to the market.

## THE SPREAD

The bid–offer spread is one of the most interesting attributes of a company's stock, although it rarely attracts much commentary. The spread tells much about the investment community's view on the company. In general, larger spreads reflect more uncertainty; while smaller spreads reflect a greater willingness of investors to transact.

The spread is anything but a constant metric. Spreads fluctuate from one trading day to the next due to the prevailing economic climate and the sentiments of investors. They also fluctuate on an intraday basis, affected by the daily movements in the markets, and the relative level of activity at different times of the day. Spreads, like stock prices, can spike during periods of market imbalances. An unusual movement in the spread can denote the beginning of a price rally or a reversal.

Spreads differ greatly based on the type of company and sector of the market. Spreads are lowest in stocks that are the most liquid, such as those in the financial sector, and are higher in the less liquid sectors, such as utility stocks. Spreads are usually greater in lower-capitalization companies, for which there are fewer investors willing to provide liquidity.

Across the globe, spreads differ greatly from region to region. Some spreads are constrained to be artificially high given the exchange's minimum tick size, as is the case on the Paris Bourse and the TSE. Stocks, however, often trade at much greater spreads than their minimum tick size. The market participants often are the determinants of the prevailing spread, reflecting both their views on the underlying risks and their costs of providing liquidity.

Transaction costs are a significant influence on the size of the spread. A more costly environment—brokerage commissions, local taxes, settlement fees—contributes to the frictional costs incurred by market makers. Market mechanisms and the regulatory environment can also introduce costs of the infrastructure and operational investment required to offer short-term liquidity. In the most liquid sectors, spreads will gravitate toward the round-trip frictional costs of the market.

Economic uncertainty, however, will remain the most influential factor in determining the spread. During market crises, such as the collapse of Lehman Brothers in October 2008, spreads across the globe were at historical highs because there were fewer participants willing to provide liquidity in the market. Spreads will always reflect the prevailing economic uncertainty, increasing in periods of crisis and decreasing with improved investor sentiments.

Market making, correspondingly, involves a great deal of risk. Any firm that accumulates inventory in a stock is subject to the risk of adverse market movements. Market makers do not expect to make money on each transaction, but rather they expect to have a sustainable investment strategy to earn profits over time. Since the marketplace is volatile, market makers must balance the costs of adverse market movements against the opportunities for short-term profits.

The new breed of niche market makers, high-frequency traders, has been playing the game based on the "law of large numbers." They are looking to make tiny profits, over and over, to compensate for the costs of unwinding risk. They do not take concentrated risk, as the traditional market makers do, but rather they have a systematic approach to providing bids and offers continuously across thousands of securities. With a portfolio view on the market, they can optimize the process of unwinding risk and hedge against the costs of adverse movements.

High-frequency trading firms' objectives are to profit on the fluctuation of liquidity in the marketplace. They focus their research on understanding the factors that influence the spread. Why are spreads smaller in the mornings than in the middle of the day? What happens to the spread on the morning of an earnings release? What's the impact of a large movement in the futures market? What happens if a correlated security has a price spike?

It is not because they haven't been successful that nobody has heard of them. Getco is reported to have achieved revenues of several hundred million in 2008, in an economic climate that nearly bankrupted the average investment firm. Nobody had heard of high-frequency trading, until recently, because they were quietly making money as an anonymous intermediary.

But, in the wake of the economic crisis, high-frequency trading has risen to the headlines. In an issue of the *Economist*, the "rise of the machines" has raised concerns among investors and regulators throughout Wall Street, claiming the success of high-frequency traders has come at the price of gouging other investors.[5] The need for speed has regulators taking an interest in knowing who are the most active investors.

## PREDATORS, SPECULATORS, OR INVESTORS

The financial community is only now finding its bearings on this new form of trading. Is high-frequency trading a form of speculation or is it an innovative investment strategy? Is it creating volatility or stabilizing the market? High-frequency trading firms have become the latest chapter in the long debate on treatment of short-term investors, presumed to be speculators until proven otherwise.

## Pinging the Book

At the heart of the controversy are the tactics used by the high-frequency firms. The type of liquidity they are bringing to the marketplace may not be beneficial to the long-term investor. One such tactic is known as "pinging the book," in which high-frequency firms submit and cancel their orders within milliseconds.

Pinging is a tactical strategy used to entice another investor into trading. Orders are submitted to an ECN and if they are not filled within a threshold of 60–80 milliseconds, they will be cancelled. The high-frequency firm is attempting to solicit hidden liquidity of investors that are passively waiting for a specific target price. If their rapid-fire orders are filled outright, the high-frequency trader has learned important information on the key price levels at which others are willing to trade.

Studies have estimated that as much as 30 percent of ECN orders are canceled within one second after they are placed. Under particular scenarios, for every single U.S. market transaction, there are hundreds of thousands of orders submitted across the various ECN venues. High-frequency firms are speculated to be the root cause of this noise.

Critics claim that high-frequency algorithms, while trying to extract information from the marketplace, entice investors to trade at prices they wouldn't have otherwise. Although this is a legitimate theoretical view, the proponents of high-frequency trading would counter with the phrase "it takes two to tango."

## Predatory Algorithms

Pinging the book is only one type of controversial tactic used by high-frequency firms. The general complaint by traditional investors is that these algorithms have taken on a "predatory" nature. High-frequency algorithms are being designed to influence how other investors trade.

Predatory algorithms try to "game" other investors into chasing the market. The basic tactic is for a high-frequency algorithm to improve the prevailing best bid (or offer) repeatedly in hopes other investors will follow. These algorithms place an order at the best bid price, and if more shares join the queue, they then place an additional order at the next best bid price, hoping more will join. Effectively, they are moving the bid price to a higher price range, without making a single transaction.

Critics claim this predatory approach is effective because of the increase in automation throughout the financial industry. Other algos, used by banks to execute their client's order, are mandated to trade at the NBBO. So if the best bid is improved, algos must follow and improve their bids in the market, regardless whether there has been a trade at the better price.[6]

The predator is believed to be preying on other algorithmic flows in the marketplace that are susceptible to manipulation. Of course, there is no evidence that a predatory algorithm can affect the market. Price movements can always be caused by long-term investors or the start of a market rally. Investors concede that these tactics are perfectly legal. But critics will claim that high-frequency traders should be flagged for unsportsmanlike conduct.

## The Rebate Structure

The most significant controversy in the high-frequency realm is that these firms are being paid to trade. They not only will earn a spread in the difference between bids and offers, but also they will earn a fee paid by the liquidity venue. The single most prevailing reason for the growth of high-frequency trading is the "rebate structure" used by ECNs, which want to attract investors.

Although there are several payment models for ECNs, the most common is a "credit-rebate structure," which awards one-quarter of a penny to the firm that provides liquidity to the marketplace. In the credit-rebate structure, ECNs make a profit from paying "liquidity providers" a credit while charging a debit to "liquidity demanders." Their rebate fees range from $0.002 to $0.0027 per share: a small fee that accumulates at high turnover levels.

A liquidity provider is the firm whose orders are hit (or lifted) in the ECN's order book. It is the firm that places a bid or offer into the queue and waits for a liquidity demander to transact at its price level. A liquidity demander is the firm that effectively removes an order from the order book by hitting a bid (seller takes the prevailing bid price) or lifting an offer (buyer takes the prevailing offer price). The ECN's credit-rebate structure is designed to entice liquidity providers to place orders into its order queue. The ECN earns money from the investors that need this liquidity.

From a theoretical perspective, the rebate structure acts as a de facto discount to the bid–offer spread because it allows investors to be more aggressive when placing orders. From a practical perspective, critics feel this has changed the playing field of investing, making it an advantageous game for the technology-centric firms.

The first firm to get its orders into the ECN queue is rewarded for providing liquidity to the market. Only the firms with state-of-the-art technology can maintain priority on their peers. The growth of high-frequency firms has made one thing clear: traditional asset managers are having a tough time keeping pace with the speed of the markets.

## THE COMPETITION FOR LIQUIDITY

The biggest supporters of high-frequency trading are believers that lower costs are better for all investors. As evidence from the Paris Bourse highlighted, lower spreads will improve liquidity by attracting diverse investment strategies, leading toward a more efficient marketplace. Few investors can dispute that the regulatory reforms, from Reg ATS through Reg NMS, have made the U.S. marketplace more competitive, and have resulted in historical lows in spreads, arguably the most influential factor of transaction costs.

High-frequency trading is a new industry that has been evolved on the back of market reforms, technology innovations, and the growing sophistication of investors. The industry accelerated after the Reg NMS rule changes in 2005, when the industry imposed best execution standards. Subsequently, there's been a rapid increase in the volume that transacts on ECNs, rather than the U.S. exchanges (see figure 7.1).

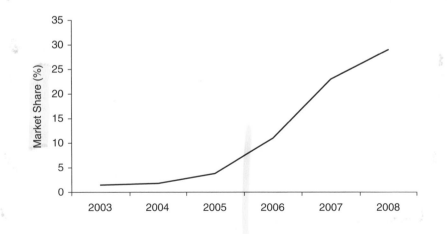

**FIGURE 7.1**   Market share of ECNs

The U.S. markets, since the end of the internet bubble, have observed average spreads to decline from 30 basis points to less than 8 basis points. High-frequency traders have not been the only investment firms putting downward pressure on spreads; but they have been doing their part in keeping spreads low throughout a worsening economic climate.

The investment community has had reason for concern during the recent market reforms. The market share of transactions by NYSE specialists has declined from 80 percent to 25 percent of total NYSE turnover since the introduction of Reg NMS. At the start of 2009, the NYSE floor had fewer than 1,200 floor traders, down from 3,000 five years beforehand.

High-frequency firms are a big driver of changing the economics of traditional investment businesses, but also they have cannibalized the role of traditional investment professionals. But, regardless of differing criticism of high-frequency traders, most investors are in agreement of a common theme: a competitive marketplace is in everyone's interests.

Competition goes beyond different investors chasing the same opportunities. It transcends the entire industry, affecting the entire food chain of market participants. Black-box firms have been responsible for one of the largest competitions in the history of the financial markets: the competition for liquidity.

The proliferation of ECNs in the past decade was the direct result of market reforms that leveled the playing field with the stock exchanges. The emergence of ECNs spawned a variety of new investment strategies, from statistical arbitrage to high-frequency trading. But, after nearly a decade from their inception, ECNs are entertaining a competitor for their liquidity—"dark pools."

Trading platforms known as dark pools are the latest innovations of technology to emerge on the global marketplace. A dark pool is an anonymous crossing network that allows institutions to hide their orders from the marketplace. Dark pools appeal to institutional investors that desire to move a large block of shares, while disseminating little information to the financial community.

Dark pools have been around for a few years. They were initially a spin-off platform from ECNs in response to regulatory reforms in 2002. Liquidnet, POSIT, and Pipeline Trading Services were among the industry's earliest dark pools, each offering differentiated implementations of crossing logic to attract investors.

The economic incentive for dark pools began to grow in 2008 due to the worsening economic climate. Investors began to trade away from ECNs, because they could lower their costs when crossing orders in dark pools. With the equity markets observing massive declines, most financial firms were losing revenue. Investment banks, in particular, were haemorrhaging their commission revenue earned from executing their client orders. Settlement costs, which were once insignificant, were now more substantial.

An investment bank reduces settlement costs when it executes in dark pools, rather than on a ECN or stock exchange. Investment banks pay away as much as 0.40 to 0.60 basis points for settlement and clearing fees on an ECN, and even more on a stock exchange. Dark pools offered investment banks the ability to "internalize" their flow; that is, cross client orders internally, when they have a buyer and a seller in the same stock. Crossing off market saves the settlement costs on two client orders.

By internalizing even a small percentage of client orders, brokers could yield large cost savings. Goldman Sachs' Sigma-X platform crossed 1.47 percent of its internal client flows in 2008.[7] This is a small proportion of total client turnover but it translates to millions of dollars of annual cost savings.

Dark pools began to offer an attractive cost advantage as the marketplace became more populated by high-frequency traders. When commissions were high and spreads were 30 basis points, investment banks had little concern for a basis point of settlement cost. The economics of the industry has gradually evolved to squeeze more frictional costs out of the food chain. Black-box firms, if anything, have heightened the industry's emphasis on the frictional effects of trading.

This new emphasis has had a strong influence throughout the industry. In particular, investment banks have started to pressure their largest vendors: the stock exchanges. Investment banks have lobbied the stock exchanges for years to reduce their fee structure. But before the formation of ECNs, stock exchanges had very little competition. Once they started losing market share to ECNs and dark pools, stock exchanges began to listen to complaints.

The European markets enjoyed the longest stretch of monopolistic rule.[8] When the European Union introduced the Markets in Financial Instruments Directive (MiFID) in November of 2007, these reforms aligned the U.K. markets with the U.S. standards, and ignited competition among the European bourses.

A year after the introduction of MiFID in Europe, Instinet's electronic commerce network, Chi-X, captured 15.7 percent of the FTSE 100 total volume. The demand for alternative execution venues in Europe has been substantial. Several venues have joined the party, Turquoise and BATS Trading Inc., to name a couple of the early entrants. The popularity of ECNs in Europe, although driven by many factors, is strongly influenced by cost pressure and the need to compete for liquidity. The LSE, the Deutsche Boerse, and Swiss Stock Exchange all announced reforms to their fee structure in 2008.

Economists and investors will debate their concerns about the impact of the high-frequency trading firms. Whether they are predators or innovators will be the topic of white papers out of academia for years to come. Despite all the skepticism, high-frequency traders are clearly the largest carnivores of transaction costs in the industry. The trends in the industry also indicate that the least heard of investors just may have the loudest voice.

In an article in the *Wall Street Journal* in March 2009 the NYSE announced that it would begin paying "rebates" to all investors proactively sending orders to the Big Board.[9] The 216-year-old exchange, notorious for protectionism, had finally succumbed to the realities of competition for liquidity in the modern electronic marketplace.

# CHAPTER 8

# The Russell Rebalance

## *Why the Market's Close Doesn't Always Reflect Our Economic Health*

T he market's closing price is one of the most relevant metrics on a public company. CEOs regularly quote their stock's closing price to employees as an update of the company's progress. For individual investors, today's closing price relative to yesterday's close represents the change in their net worth. For corporations, the closing price is used throughout the mutual fund industry to valuate a fund; it's also used by conglomerates to value their holdings. Our interpretation of our net worth and the health of our economy is largely influenced by the closing prices of our major global markets.

On days with key economic reports, such as the Federal Reserve Bank's release of quarterly announcements of gross domestic product, the emphasis on the market close is particularly heightened. How investors interpret a key piece of economic information is influential to our perspective on the prevailing climate, and the market close helps us differentiate good news from bad. After the release of unemployment data, if the market closes in positive territory, we interpret investors' sentiments to have improved.

In most global markets, the market close is the busiest time of the day. On an average day, the final minutes of the trading session can represent anywhere from 5–10 percent of the day's trading activity. Institutional investors, even if liquidity were sufficient to complete their orders in the morning, will hold off until the market close, to participate in the most active period of the day. This reflects the significance of the market closing price.

On particular days of the year, the activity in the market close is accentuated. As much as an average day's volume will transact in the closing moments of the trading session. These days are known as "special trading days," on which the volume is abnormally large.

On an average day in the global equity markets, typically 5–7 percent of the market capitalization will change hands due to natural investor flows. Long-term investors will rebalance their weightings, buying into new positions and decreasing holdings in other stocks; pension funds will have new investors or redemptions to recalibrate; hedge funds will speculate on particular opportunities; retail investors may buy into a blue-chip stock. A few percentage points of the free float of publicly available shares are the normal level of trading activity.

On special trading days, as much as 20 percent of the market capitalization has been known to transact in particular stocks, and this trading activity is largely around the market close. Special trading days are not driven by the release of economic information; rather, they are caused by specific market events that accentuate the need for liquidity on the part of particular subsets of investors.

In the U.S. markets, one of the most common special days is known as the "triple witching," when index futures, index options, and stock options expire simultaneously. This occurs four times a year, every third Friday in March, June, September, and December. Volumes are pronounced because derivative traders roll their positions from one contract to the next.

In Japan, stock option expiry dates occur at the end of every month, known as the "SQ date." Trading volumes and stock market volatility are heavily pronounced on these days. Price swings twice the average day are an expected byproduct of the demand for liquidity by the derivative community.

Holidays, on a global perspective, also represent special trading days in the sense of their influence on trading activity. The National Stock Exchange of India is the only market in the world to be open on January 1. Interpreting the market close of India's blue-chip stocks on the New Year may need a footnote to explain the absence of foreigners.

Black-box firms are particularly sensitive to understanding the local nuances of special trading days around the globe. Abnormal volume activity adversely affects the calibration of their models. Vast amounts of their quantitative research efforts are spent on understanding the volume distribution around these local market events.

There is no more significant special trading event than the last Friday of June, during the annual "Russell Rebalance." In the U.S. markets, the closing prices on the last day of June are the most relevant to one of the largest group of investors: index funds.

The demand for liquidity by index funds benchmarked to the Russell indexes, has spawned one of the biggest black-box events of the years.

Billions of dollars in black-box algorithms are chasing the same signal: the close price.

## THE RUSSELL RECONSTITUTION

The most active trading day of the year in U.S. markets occurs without exception during the last week of June when the Russell Investment Group rebalances its indexes during an annual event known as the "Russell Reconstitution" or simply the "Russell Rebalance." More shares change hands in the last minute of Nasdaq's closing session during the reconstitution than in an average month on all the Latin American markets combined.

The reconstitution is a heavily anticipated day as asset managers benchmarked to the Russell indexes seek to reconfigure their portfolios to match the new configurations announced by the Russell Investment Group. Asset managers tracking the indexes must buy the new stocks to be included in the indexes and must sell the stocks to be excluded. The stocks targeted for inclusion and exclusion will experience massive accelerated volume during the rebalance, often multiples of several days of their average trading volume.

Index funds have been around for three decades. John Bogle of the Vanguard Group pioneered this asset class with the flagship First Index Investment Trust in 1975, a fund targeted to match the performance of the S&P 500 index. This fund was later renamed the Vanguard 500 Index Fund and crossed the $100 billion milestone in November of 1999. Since their inception in the 1970s, index funds have been a huge success with retail investors given their low cost and their straightforward investment strategy. The merits of index funds are well understood: an index fund offers the return of a broad market index, without paying the higher management fees of a comparable mutual fund.

The past decade has observed a massive growth of assets invested in index funds. Investors can select from every broad market index, such as the S&P 500, Nasdaq 100, and Dow Jones Industrial Average. As of 2008, there were $4.4 trillion of assets invested in index funds. More refined index products became available through exchange-traded funds (ETFs), which track particular industries and sub-sectors.[1]

Barclays Global Investors (BGI) has grown into the largest asset management firm with its iShare ETF brand. State Street Global Advisors followed with the formation of S&P Spiders, which track the nine subsectors of the S&P index. As of 2008, there were 680 ETFs in the U.S.

alone, representing $610 billion in assets and covering every imaginable sector or region: health care, energy, water, manufacturing, and so on.

Although there are many different ways of implementing an index fund, the basic approach is a "passive" tracking strategy. In a passive approach, the index fund simply buys all the holdings of the index in weights consistent with the actual index. A passive S&P 500 index fund would hold all 500 underlying stocks in the exact weights of the index. Investors thus receive the same market return of the S&P 500, less the index fund's management fee.

During an index weight change event, such as the Russell reconstitution, the index fund must rebalance its holdings to reflect the new weights. Unfortunately for the index fund managers, they have much competition between other index funds that also need to recalibrate. Each index fund wants to trade at the same time: the market close.

## THE IMPACT OF TRACKING RISK

Since the investment objective of an index fund is to track the index, any deviation from the true index represents underperformance. The difference between the index performance and the fund performance is known as "tracking error," and in the case of traditional index funds it's the most relevant metric to validate the quality of the index fund manager. Index funds attempt to stay within a tight range of the index, such as a 0.50 percent range within a year. A wider tracking error would be a deterrent for investors of these funds.

The Russell Rebalance, on the last trading day of every June, represents the most significant impact to an index manager's tracking risk. It needs to buy the inclusion stocks and sell the exclusion stocks at exactly the market closing price. The closing price is the benchmark for managers because the Russell Investment Group applies the closing prices to derive the value of its indexes. Any deviation from the closing price will erode its fund's annual performance.

Its dilemma is that there is insufficient liquidity to trade precisely at the market close. Given the amount of assets tracking the same indexes, there is an exceptionally large demand for liquidity. The demand for liquidity usually outweighs the normal trading activity in the underlying stocks targeted for inclusion and exclusion. An index fund can offset this risk by trading earlier than the market close, but then it incurs underperformance when deviating from the closing price.

The Russell 2000 index funds, in particular, represent the most pronounced demanders of liquidity during the Russell Reconstitution.

The Russell 2000 index is the most widely recognized index for small-capitalization stocks in the U.S. markets. It contains the smallest 2,000 stocks held by the Russell 3000 index and represents 7 percent of the market capitalization of U.S. stocks.

The average firm in the Russell 2000 has a market capitalization of less than $1 billion, and most stocks fall in the range of a few hundred million. The demand for liquidity can be very pronounced in the tail of small-capitalization stocks. The Russell Rebalance is a competition for index fund managers that demand liquidity in the same stocks, which are targeted for inclusion and exclusion.[2]

The aggregate demands of all the Russell 2000 index trackers are substantial. In 2006, it was estimated that $62 billion of assets were tracking the Russell 2000 index. If a small-capitalization stock targeted for inclusion was to represent a 0.1 percent weight in the Russell 2000 index, there would be $62 million of liquidity demanded by index-tracking funds. Even if this stock had a market capitalization of as much as $1 billion, index funds would require several days of its average daily volume; and they would all want to trade at the market close.

The demand for liquidity creates massive volume expansion around the U.S. market close during the Russell Rebalance. On an average day in U.S. markets, 5–10 percent of the stock's daily volume might transact in the closing five minutes of trading; on the Russell, the stock's volume is in the range of 30–50 percent in the closing moments (see figure 8.1).

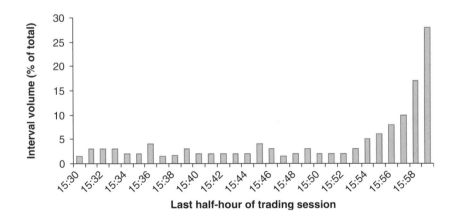

**FIGURE 8.1**  Volume expansion on Russell Rebalance

Index fund managers offset their execution risk by engaging in "guaranteed" risk trades with investment banks. For a fixed commission, the index fund locks in the close price, and the investment bank's black-box strategies will manage the competition for liquidity.

## THE GUARANTEED TRADE

Index funds outsource the execution risk on rebalance days to investment banks through "principal transactions." Investment banks offer index fund managers a "guaranteed close" price on their portfolios in exchange for a commission. This is a lucrative opportunity for investment banks given that the commissions earned from a single index fund could be upward of several million dollars.

The investment bank is taking risk when offering principal transactions. The bank earns a commission on the transaction, but is exposed to the market movements because it has guaranteed the client a pre-agreed price. The bank typically will lose money when unwinding the position in the market. The difference between the guaranteed price and its execution price is their slippage. If the investment bank earns 25 basis points commission but loses 15 basis points relative the close benchmark, then it has retained 10 basis points. On a hundred-million-dollar transaction, it would retain $1 million of revenue.

Principal trades (or risk trades) serve a valued purpose to index managers. The investment bank is providing liquidity to the fund by allowing it to unwind a large position in one single transaction. The index fund pays a commission for receiving a guaranteed price and for outsourcing the execution risk to the investment bank.

The "guaranteed close" price is the pre-agreed price used by index funds on the Russell Rebalance. They want to lock in the market close, for a fixed commission, to minimize tracking risk. These deals are usually negotiated days before the Russell Rebalance.

The unique incentive for guaranteed trades is that the investment bank is agnostic to the direction of the market. They can make money whether the stocks are up 10 percent or down 10 percent. Their objective is to minimize the slippage from the actual market close. Their fate is decided by their ability to forecast volume accurately in the Russell's constituent stock changes.

A guaranteed close trade is a risky trade because price volatility can be excessive. Abnormal price movements are common during rebalance events, and investment banks can observer slippage in double-digit percentages from their benchmark close. They might earn several million in commissions, but lose 10 times as much during the unwinding.

The Russell Rebalance is a particularly risky trade because the volume of shares trading is abnormal. Investment banks will try to estimate the demand for liquidity based on the size of the known traditional (or passive) index funds. Since traditional index funds usually hold all the index constituents in line with the actual index weight, investment banks will begin with that as a reference.

Investment banks will formulate a model of the expected volume distribution during the closing minutes. Since the demand for shares is too much to leave until the final minutes of market close, the investment bank will estimate the impact of trading before the market close, say 15 minutes, and work the orders into the market close. They calibrate black-box execution strategies specifically for this event.

From a quantitative investor's perspective, the Russell Rebalance is the best real-world application of numerical optimization. Since several hundred stocks are targeted for inclusion and exclusion into the Russell 2000, it's a unique demonstration of portfolio optimization. The bank's objective is to minimize slippage on the portfolio as a whole, not just on each particular name, and therefore they use a combination of pre-hedging strategies to model the relationship between correlated securities.

The "Russell Trade" is a very competitive trade among investment banks for one reason: size matters. A bank stands a better chance of minimizing slippage if it has a greater share of the market. The advantages of size are twofold: more likelihood of offsetting client orders so that they can cross off market at the exact benchmark price; and lower slippage if they are a larger share of the market turnover.

Investment banks will lobby index funds for their rebalance trades. The larger investment banks with U.S. operations, Morgan Stanley, Deutsche Bank, UBS, and Goldman Sachs, may each command more than $10 billion of portfolio orders during the Russell.

Black-box algorithms are the engines working behind the curtains to optimize and to unwind the positions: billions of dollars, all chasing the market close.

## THE RUSSELL EFFECT

Economists have researched and reported on price discrepancies that arise due to the competition for liquidity in the Russell Reconstitution. Academic studies have found that stocks added to the Russell index have a positive price movement following the announcement of their inclusion, and then experience a reversal in the days following the rebalance. For stocks excluded from the index, the opposite is true.

In a study by the Russell Investment Group, the additions to the Russell 2000 index were shown to gain on average 1.46 percent of excess return between the announcement date to the rebalance day, and then reverse on average 0.83 percent. These characteristic patterns in the price impact are known as the "Russell Effect" (see figure 8.2).

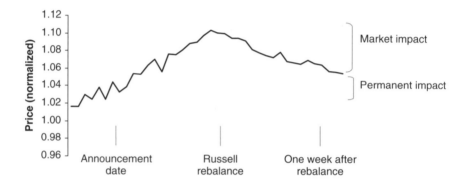

**FIGURE 8.2**   The Russell Effect

The Russell Effect has been debated as attributable, in part, to index membership effects that raise the profile of stocks included in the index.[3] These companies are off the radar before they are included in the index but they usually observe four or five writing analysts taking up their coverage when they are in. The temporary price impacts are assumed to be the effects of supply and demand among the index funds competing for liquidity. In either case, the price swings create both momentum and reversal trading opportunities for speculators, and this is why the annual Russell Trade is heavily anticipated.

The heydays of the Russell Rebalance were in the 1990s during the initial rise in prominence of index-tracking funds. In those days, the top-tier investment banks' revenues from principal risk trades were $20–$30 million. At that time, the Russell participants were a small group of well-known index funds. This made forecasting supply and demand a more straightforward process. But the participants began to change over the years.

Index funds themselves began to diversify. The early pioneers of index funds were predominately the vanilla implementation of passive managers in the major indexes. Later on, index funds have taken on more active styles, such as improved indexing and synthetic indexing. These style of index funds engage in market timing and in tweaking rebalance strategies to improve slightly upon the index performance. They are not constrained to hold all the index constituents in precise alignment with the index weights.

Hedge funds have also been cognizant of the Russell Effect. One hedge fund strategy is to speculate on the inclusions before the announcement by the Russell Investment Group. Hedge funds that successfully pick the new inclusions or exclusions can take a position in the stock, before the announcement date, and unwind during the rebalance period. Hedge funds have been large speculators in recent years.

The effect of the interaction of different investment strategies has been observed in the decay of the price anomalies. Economists have noted that the Russell Effect has diminished, year on year, from 2000 onward.[4] The new inclusions in the Russell 2000 index used to observe an excess price return of 12.7 percent from the time of the announcement to the rebalance day; by 2007, the excess returns of new inclusions had all but disappeared (see figure 8.3).

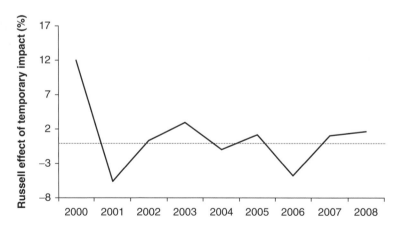

**FIGURE 8.3** Diminishing returns of Russell Trade

1990s, the Russell Trade was a very lucrative business opportunity for investment banks. The top-tier banks earned $20–$30 million
in a single day. Subsequently, the competition between different investment strategies has arbitraged away the margins of the Russell Trade.
The markets, effectively, have become more efficient as a result of
increased competition.

## THE CLOSING PRICE

Black-box trading is never more pronounced than on "special" trading
days, such as the Russell Rebalance. Algorithms could possibly dictate
100 percent of the day's trading activity in the final moments of the
U.S. markets as they compete for liquidity. Special trading days are
not isolated to the U.S. markets or index rebalance events. Global
markets experience a similar liquidity competition during the biannual
rebalancing of the MSCI World indexes, managed by MSCI Barra Inc.
The MSCI rebalances occur in July and November and have a ripple
effect throughout global markets from Germany to Sao Paulo.

The prominence of index-tracking funds has grown into a global
theme. Any change to a major industry benchmark, whether the Hang
Seng Index or Australia's All Ordinary Index, will ignite a similar
competition for liquidity. Investors have come to accept the periodic
disturbances of abnormal stock prices.

The market close is one of the most relevant metrics on the health
of a company; but the close is also the most susceptible to supply
and demand imbalances. The market's closing price, for short periods,
can deviate from the sentiments of investment community. During
the Russell Rebalance, traditional mutual funds may represent only
10 percent of the volume in particular stocks, despite being a top-10
holder.

Although the market close price has great significant throughout the
industry, there is very little consistency on the mechanisms that define
how the close price is calculated. Some markets use closing auctions
to minimize volatility; others use the last market transaction in the
trading session; while others use an average price across the last few
minutes.

The diversity of market mechanisms for how an exchange determines the closing price is actually no surprise. Economists and market
regulators have few references for evaluating the best structure to

minimize price volatility.[5] Auctions or no auctions, wild price swings are common in all global markets.

Excessive volatility is a growing concern. Some regional markets have introduced upward and downward price barriers, such as a 7 percent limit-up constraint, which suspends trading for the day. Although intuitive, price throttles do not resolve the imbalances of supply and demand. On special trading days, the market close says less about the health of our economy, and more about the demographics of investors.

# CHAPTER 9

# The Ecology of the Marketplace

## Whatever Happened to the Buy-and-Hold Investor?

The "ecology" of the financial markets is a term borrowed from biology to describe the relationships between investors and their environment. It is an appropriate analogy because just as ecologists study the impact of various species on their ecosystem, economists study the impact of investment strategies on the marketplace. There are many parallels between biological systems and the financial markets.

When Europeans brought rabbits to Australia in the 18th century, there were devastating effects on the ecosystem, leading to the extinction of many orchards and plant species. In a similar light, when the Australian Stock Exchange eliminated the dissemination of real-time market share information to its member firms in 2005, there were significant declines in market share for the local brokers, such as Macquarie Bank, because of the elimination of their information advantage on the foreign investors. Any subtle change in the market structure can have a profound impact on the population of the market participants.

Economists believe that the financial markets will remain in a prolonged period of instability if there is not equilibrium by the participants. In an ecosystem, if one species of the population is too abundant, than the food supply will be scarce. Similarly, in finance, if there are too many investors employing the same strategy, then the profit margins will be thin. Instability is the byproduct of the investors' competition for profits. Each trading strategy will influence the market price and, in turn, influence another trading strategy.

In a publication by Doyle Farmer, founder of the Prediction Company, entitled "Market Force, Ecology, and Evolution," he simulated how different types of investment strategies had unique influences on the marketplace.[1] In his research, Farmer simulated how value investors can introduce reverse auto-correlation (i.e. snapback effects) due to moving the market away from its equilibrium when they transact. Trend followers, on the other hand, introduce positive auto-correlation (i.e. momentum) by participating in market movements and increasing the rally. The relationship between value investors and trend-followers can thus achieve equilibrium in the market, by offsetting each other's influence.

Over the long term, the effects between trading strategies are more complicated than their short-term contributions. Trend followers, for instance, may increase the momentum in the marketplace by riding on the latest hot stocks, but they will introduce reversals in the long term by chasing false rallies. Stock markets can observe prolonged periods of disequilibrium because of the influences of competing investment strategies. Boom–bust cycles are the byproduct.

The interaction between investment strategies can have adverse effects on the stability of the market. John Campbell and Robert Shiller were among the first economists to simulate this market dynamic, which they denoted as "excess volatility." Evidence from historical market data suggests that, while prices track values over the long term, large deviations are the rule rather than the exception. In other words, fundamental valuations of stocks and their prices do not track one another (see figure 9.1).

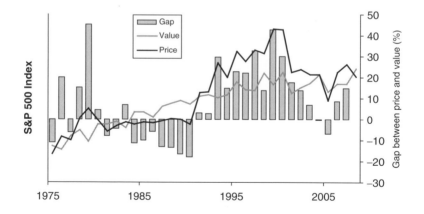

**FIGURE 9.1** The deviation of value and price

The concept of equilibrium, although central to economics, is difficult to study because the ecology of the market is always changing. Different strategies are born, prosper, and disappear; few metrics are available to track the effects of a particular strategy on its contribution to the price dynamics of the marketplace. Economists have few metrics to infer whether trend followers or value investors dominate the market at a particular moment.

The proliferation of black-box strategies has been one of the most profound influences on the equilibrium of the marketplace. Black-box firms, for a variety of reasons, have become one of the most predominate sources of liquidity in the marketplace. The catalysts for this evolution in the ecology of the financial markets have less to do with the success of black-box trading as much as they have to do with the economics of the buy-and-hold investor. Advancements in technology, changes in regulations, and commission pressure have all played a part in the displacement of the largest population of investors, the buy-and-hold strategy.

## THE CASH BUSINESS

After the internet bubble burst, there was a joke floating around Wall Street to characterize the return of MBAs that had joined startup internet ventures: "They were all looking for B2B opportunities—back-to-banking." There has only ever been one surefire industry that offers lucrative bonuses regardless of the economic climate and that is the investment banking industry. Even in recessions, institutional clients and corporations still need advice on how to weather the financial turmoil and what is their best investment strategy.

One of the most consistently lucrative professions is the sales and trading division of investment banks, because clients continue to trade in all economic cycles. In a bear-market environment, the concentration of order flows with their most valued investment banks is even more pronounced. With fewer commissions to pay for advisory services, clients prefer to consolidate their business with the banks they value the most, rather than distribute across a long tail of smaller firms. The "cash business" has historically been a profitable business throughout the ups and downs of the economy.

The cash business is the name given to the customer trading business in investment banking. It's inclusive of all commission revenue generated on client equity transactions, otherwise known as secondary market transactions. The lingo "cash" originated because stock market transactions are physically settled in cash transfers from the client to the broker's custodian, unlike futures, swaps, or option transactions, which are settled on the client's margin accounts. The cash business, more practically, represents all the facets of the secondary coverage business such as equity research, sales trading, generalist and specialist sales, and trade execution.

The cash desk often benefited by receiving large order flows from institutional clients given their dependency on investment banks for a range of services. The commissions paid on trade execution by asset managers encapsulated payment for all the services provided by the investment banks; equity research, corporate access, sales coverage, and trading. Commissions are assumed to be rewards for services provided by sales and trading professionals.

When a portfolio manager receives service from a broker, such as a research publication or an invitation to an investor conference, he or she pays for these services with the commissions generated on his or her portfolio's execution. The portfolio manager directs commissions to the brokers he or she values the most in terms of research or sales coverage. The breadth and intensity of the services provided by the broker are a function of the client's commission revenues: the larger clients will receive full-service coverage.[2]

There is nothing more oversubscribed on a Wall Street dealing floor than commission revenue. If a client places an order to purchase $10 million of British Petroleum there will be no shortage of client coverage teams to lobby for recognition of the commission revenue: a senior research analyst will be quick to highlight his or her publication of a recent report on the oil sector and key themes he or she identified ahead of the street; the client's sales coverage will mention a recent dinner with the senior portfolio manager and highlight the great rapport they have built with the client over the years; the cash trader who managed the order's execution will quote how he or she has successfully timed the market over the past month, bettering the sector averages on his or her client's trade flows. The few thousand dollars of commission are divided up pretty quickly on a dealing floor.

The portfolio manager's payment model varies greatly from firm to firm, and commission payments are not easily attributable to a particular service. If a portfolio manager was to attend a four-day tour of factories in eastern China, he or she likely will be chaperoned by a broker who arranges the trip's itinerary and coordinates meetings with senior management. The broker may act as a concierge, coordinating the client's hotel bookings, transportation, and dinner reservations. The broker may not directly pay for any of the client's expenses, but the broker provides much attention to meet the client's needs and make the trip fruitful. Likely a senior sales representative will chaperone the client, make introductions and perhaps translate Mandarin when necessary.

How then is the broker rewarded for his or her efforts? Should he or she expect to receive the portfolio manager's orders in Chinese securities in the coming weeks? In practice, there is very seldom a direct relationship between service and commission payments because clients segregate their research and execution activities.

It's often frustrating for a sales professional when he or she has provided intense service to a client and has not received a trade in the affiliated stock or sector. However, research and execution services are highly segregated within mutual funds for regulatory reasons as well as conflicts of interest. When a broker chaperones a portfolio manager on a tour of Eastern Europe, the broker is just as likely to be reciprocated with a commission in a Brazilian stock as a Polish stock. The portfolio manager does not direct his or her firm's execution.

Research services are a similar story. A telecommunications research analyst covering Sony Ericsson may engage in a two-hour conference call with the portfolio manager, providing in-depth knowledge on the earnings outlook of the particular stock, yet never receive an order in that name for the week, month, or quarter. The analyst's efforts have not fallen on deaf ears, rather the fund manager's payment model is completely segregated from his or her execution business. The fund manager has little or no knowledge of, let alone influence over, the routing of the daily trade flows to the pool of brokers.

Portfolio managers reward brokers through an internal broker review. They vote and rank brokerage services and this process leads to rewarding those brokers with the appropriate share of their portfolio's execution. If a portfolio manager commands a $1 billion portfolio, he or she may generate several million dollars of commissions throughout the year—his or her internal broker reviews will rank the brokers and pay them in proportion to the overall rank. The #1 ranking broker may earn several millions of commission from a top-tier institutional client.

The client's review process must encompass all the different facets of the sell-side service. Its review must weight the value of access to corporate management during a country tour as compared to a quality research publication on the oil sector. Their review must differentiate the value of timely news and market color from the sales trading desk versus the availability of a prominent research analyst around a company earnings announcement. Their vote must consider all facets of the sell-side services and reward each contributor with the commissions generated on its transactions in British Petroleum and the like.

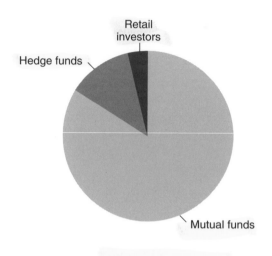

**FIGURE 9.2**    1990s distribution of turnover

The sustainability of their broker review process is correspondingly dependent on the underlying economics of the industry. If the commissions paid to brokers are on the decline then the sell-side services will also be impacted. Intensity of sales coverage, tours of eastern China, and invitations to investors' conferences are increasingly difficult for the brokers to justify.

In the 1990s, the cash business would have represented as much as 80 percent of the equity division's revenue for an investment bank (see figure 9.2). Subsequently, the cash business model has suffered under a variety of economic stresses: commission pressure, regulatory reforms, technology developments, and industry trends have all played a role in reducing the dominance of the cash business as the largest contributor of market liquidity.

Cash is not king any more because commissions are not as lofty as they used to be and because the demand for services has only increased. A cost structure inclusive of field trips, investment conferences, and research publications has made the traditional commission business a marginally profitable business for most full-service investment banks.

The ecology of the marketplace, consequently, has evolved away from a large population of buy-and-hold investors toward a diverse variety of liquidity providers.

# TRENDS IN ORDER SEGMENTATION

The commissions received from cash equity transactions each year are in excess of several billion dollars for most global investment banks. In the U.S. alone there are more than 10,000 registered investment managers, each dependent on research, sales, and trading services from the banking community. A global investment bank may have active relationships with 2,000–3,000 asset management firms and countless individual contacts with their analysts, associates, and portfolio managers.

On an aggregate basis, an investment bank may have tens of thousands of person-to-person interactions between its coverage professionals and its client universe throughout the course of a year. Each one of those interactions, presumably, contributes to earning commissions. Accounting for the commissions can be a challenging process, however.

How clients pay commissions to their service providers is not limited to one product. There are three main execution portals for stock trading. Clients can send single orders to an investment bank's cash trading desk, they can send a basket of orders to the portfolio desk, or they can self-trade through the bank's electronic trading products.

Before the advent of electronic trading, the staple throughout the financial industry was the traditional telephone. Clients would place their orders by phone to the bank's sales trading coverage professional. Only a decade ago, the phone (or fax machine) would represent 90 percent of how orders were placed.

The maturity of electronic trading platforms and the bursting of the internet bubble were arguably the two catalysts to transform how clients would place their orders. Under the economic pressures of the post-internet recession, most institutional clients would look to improve the efficiency of their trading desks with the adoption of technology. They would begin to segregate their orders across the different execution portals (cash, portfolio, and electronic trading) to improve the scalability of their trading desks and to better their commission distribution.

The process of "order segmentation" is an asset manager's way of organizing a list of orders for the most appropriate execution venue. A large global asset manager may have a few hundred stock orders to execute each day, on behalf of its teams of portfolio managers. Segmentation, in its simplest form, is how an asset manager organizes their orders into "high" touch or "low" touch buckets. Large orders, such as a $10 million order to buy Google, would be denoted as a high-touch order because the size is potentially sufficient to move the market. A high-touch order thus merits the attention of a trader to work the execution manually. Low-touch orders, conversely, are deemed small enough not to represent significant demand for liquidity and are suitable for automation. These orders are ideal for portfolio trading or electronic trading venues.

Historically, high-touch order flows would have represented the bulk of a investment bank's execution business. At least 70–80 percent of its total commission business would have been received through the cash desk. After the internet bubble, asset managers' use of low-touch venues has increased year on year so as to skew the economics of the business.[3]

Low-touch venues offered great improvements to the execution process. Portfolio trading allowed asset managers to organize their list of orders that have high degree of covariance (i.e. correlated sectors) and would benefit from being worked collectively in a portfolio trade, rather than as a set of individual orders. Electronic trading products, such as vwap algorithms, were well suited for automation of small-order execution, thus allowing the asset manager to concentrate its attentions on its high-touch orders that demanded liquidity.

High-touch orders, consequently, have been on a decline each year for the past decade. The cash desk's percentage of execution flows would decline to less than 50 percent of total flows by 2008 (see figure 9.3).

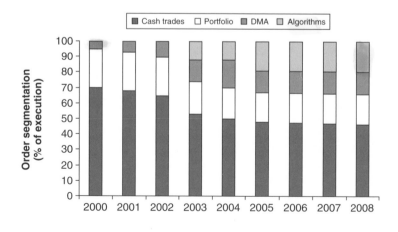

**FIGURE 9.3**   Execution by business line

The change in demographics of customer execution venues had a profound effect on the cost structure of full-service customer trading. Settlement, clearing, and infrastructure costs were growing on the back of massive volume expansion; but at the same time, gross revenues as a function of trading volumes were declining. Estimates of realized blended rates, the total of commission revenues per trading volume, were compressed from the range of 30 basis points to 12 basis points (see figure 9.4).

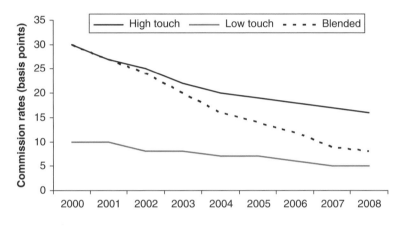

**FIGURE 9.4**   Trends in full-service commissions

Although the customer business still remains a multibillion-dollar industry for top-tier investment banks, the profitability of the business has changed dramatically. And so has the informational advantage of any particular bank. Asset managers' adoption of order segmentation has transformed the nature of liquidity. There are fewer large orders consolidated with a particular investment bank. This effect has eroded the informational advantages of investment banks and has facilitated the growth of new types of liquidity providers.

## BEST-EXECUTION MANDATES

Not only has the erosion of order flows away from investment banks been a function of the economics of their clients, but also the regulatory environment has accelerated the redistribution of execution. Regulatory reforms related to "best execution" have had a strong influence on breaking down the consolidation of execution within any single firm.

Best-execution mandates are a series of regulator reforms that require an asset manager to use the best-execution venue for its order execution. In the context of competing execution venues, such as ECNs and exchanges, best-execution guidelines require an asset manager to execute its orders on the venue that publishes the best available price. The manager cannot buy shares at $30.0 on the NYSE if they are available on an ECN at $29.5.

More broadly, best-execution regulations are targeted at the conflicts of interest within investment banks. During the late 1990s, there were a variety of market infractions that created an image problem for Wall Street investment banks with regulators; most prominently, equity research was felt biased toward the banks' interests, rather than their clients'.

In the wake of the Enron and WorldCom collapses, financial regulators believed that these accounting scandals were prolonged because the investment banking community was reluctant to publish negative reports on the firms that they covered. Although the banks were responsible for publishing research on these firms, they were also trying to lure investment banking commissions from these firms.

In the aftermath of these scandals, the SEC was empowered to reduce conflicts of interests that arose during investment banks marketing of their lucrative corporate finance mandates. The *Sarbanes-Oxley Act 2002*, also known as the *Public Company Accounting Reform and Investor Protection Act 2002*, is a U.S. federal law enacted on July 30, 2002 in response to these accounting scandals, which cost investors billions of dollars.

The legislation established improved standards for all U.S. public company boards, management, and public accounting firms. Predominately, it was intended to restore public confidence in the capital markets by segregating church and state. The guidelines mitigated conflicts of interest within investment banks such as the roles of securities analysts, who make buy and sell recommendations on company stocks and bonds, and investment bankers, who help provide company's loans or handle mergers and acquisitions.

In the peak of the Nasdaq bubble, analysts' forecasts at times were 70 percent "buy" ratings. There were few, if any, negative reports published on the firms analysts covered. The accounting scandals of Enron and WorldCom highlighted to investors that analysts' recommendations weren't always unbiased.

Sarbanes-Oxley was the first phase of a tougher regulatory environment to ensure the independence of the research product. Investment banks were required to segregate their research analyst and banking teams, restricting the two from interacting or pitching for investment banking business together.

Research departments subsequently became more closely aligned with the equity trading floors after the implementation of Sarbanes-Oxley. This was only the beginning of how best-execution mandates would change how trading commissions were earned.

## Unbundled Research

Even with the segregation of equity research and investment banking, there was more to the story of conflicts of interest. Regulators believed investors were adversely affected when fund managers awarded commissions (for execution business) to brokers simply on the basis of their research product. Investors, in their view, wouldn't receive the best price on their execution activity when the trades were not routed to the best-execution venue.

The assumption was that a broker with the best research product might not have the best execution platform. Regulators were concerned about the impact of fund managers awarding execution flows for access to senior research analysts, corporate meetings, investor conferences, or allocations of public offerings. The brokerage business model that relied on research and advisory services to be paid out of trading commissions had an inherent conflict of interest in that investors didn't receive the best execution.

The U.K.'s Financial Services Authority (FSA) was the most aggressive in tackling this conflict of interest. Its solution was "unbundling," the segregation of research commissions and execution commissions. The FSA's first step was a mandate implemented on July 1, 2006 to all FSA-regulated asset managers requiring disclosure of their commission payments for execution and research. If an asset manager was paying 15 basis points to execute with Goldman Sachs' cash desk, the asset manager must disclose the percentage that was to pay for research and the percentage for execution; such as eight basis points research and seven basis points execution.

Although this was only a subtle stepping stone, the FSA was navigating asset managers toward distinguishing research and execution as difference services. The additional mandate of segregated commissions would be the first phase in enticing asset managers toward hard-dollar payments for research services. A segregated payment model would effectively eliminate a broker's ability to earn execution orders merely based on its relationship with the client.

Although unbundling had been discussed in financial circles for years, the July 2006 regulation changes truly ignited a buzz in the industry for U.K. investment managers. Initially, it was even very challenging for investment managers to define "research" services. Fund managers have a vast array of dialog and contact with their brokerage counterparts; investment mangers receive hardcopy research reports, they speak with sales generalists and sector specialists, they have direct contact with analysts and corporate management, they are copied on countless daily email distributions, they attend investor conferences, and they often receive intraday market color and updates on their key holdings.

A large investment house may have more than 200 broker relationships on a global scale for their advisory service. Macroeconomic research, sector analysis, detailed company reports, investor conferences, corporate meetings, and the like can put a very large footprint across the brokerage community. In a bundled commission structure, local-country brokers in Latin America have historically been paid out of directed execution flows. Unbundling programs or commission sharing arrangements (CSAs) would be a new paradigm for the industry.

The industry's dilemma was on the valuation of research products. How was an investment manager to value an investor conference in Mumbai against a research analyst's macroeconomic publication on gross domestic product projections in Poland? The traditional payment models in a "bundled" commission structure were diverse but they all encompassed a formal or informal ranking system of brokerage services.

A client's #1 ranking broker may be awarded 15–20 percent of its total commission payouts, while the next layer of #3 to #5 might earn 7–9 percent, and so on. The tail of small, local brokers that coordinate the occasional corporate meeting or provide a recommendation on a small-capitalization stock may be rewarded with a one-off trade to compensate for the service, earning less than 0.5 percent of a client's commission pool.

The bundled structure was often ambiguous and that was to the benefit of the asset manager—let the brokers compete and lobby for better rankings. A #1 ranking was a big carrot dangled out to the sellside coverage teams, regardless of the level of commissions earned. Unbundling, however, would ignite a new paradigm in the industry, a migration toward "à la carte" payment models and more clearly defined commissions for specific types of service.

## Boutique Research

The FSA guidelines in July 2006 were only the starting point of the new business model for full-service brokers. The SEC adopted similar guidelines in January 2007 with the relaxation of Section 28e "safe harbor," governing the usage of money manager's commission dollars. The relaxation of section 28e empowered clients to make third-party payments to unregistered investment dealers. The SEC's reforms were creating a level playing field for boutique research firms to earn commission from fund managers through hard-dollar payments.

The demand for independent research was strong and had been growing moderately with institutional asset managers. Goldman Sachs was most aggressive in participating in the demand for investment research, and, in 2007, it announced the formation of new venture, Hudson Street Services, a platform to deliver boutique research to their institutional client base.[4] Hudson Street operates as a intermediary to provide clients with access to independent research providers.

There had always been a gap in the research provided by Wall Street and that demanded by their clients. The equity research departments of Wall Street's big bracket investment banks typically concentrated on large capitalization securities where most commissions were earned. As a result 60 percent of public securities are not actively covered by the big-bracket firms.[5] Independent research firms and investment boutiques evolved to cover the stocks orphaned by Wall Street.

The SEC's relaxation of safe harbor guidelines was the catalyst to the proliferation of independent research. Before the rule changes, all equity research had to be remunerated through trading commissions, thus inhibiting any independent firms that were not registered broker–dealers. The SEC's rule changes paved the way for the growth of boutique research and added another layer of competition to the Wall Street's equity research departments, furthering the legacy relationship of consolidated high-touch cash execution within investment banks with the largest research departments.

The effects of the unbundling movement are only at their infancy. Industry surveys estimate that less than 5 percent of all U.K. fund managers have implemented wholesale CSAs for procurement of their advisory services. A wholesale program implies the client pays its research providers with hard-dollar payments entirely, such as negotiating full-service research for a $10 million annual fee. In all likelihood, it would take several years for asset managers truly to renovate their procurement of research services and for the industry to observe the impacts.

The influences of unbundling may be a significant change to the business model of investment banks' sales and trading. Unbundling provides a major incentive for asset managers because it allows them to procure independent research at a fixed rate, unlike market-to-market with traditional bundled commissions. It also accommodates clients to increase their research providers without increasing their execution footprint. The industry could observe a massive growth of boutique/independent research on the back of the unbundling movement. And the cost structure of full-service brokers will face further pressure.

Best-execution mandates have been further catalysts to change the nature of liquidity in the marketplace. They have broken down the relationships between research and execution, thus eroding a bank's ability to consolidate flows from a particular asset manager. Correspondingly, the large block orders are now further fragmented across the execution providers. How institutional investors acquire their demands for liquidity is not the way it used to be.

## THE EVOLUTION OF LIQUIDITY

Each and every market reform, regardless of the intention, has a corresponding impact on the ecology of the marketplace. Some of the consequences are intended while others are unintended. In the past decade, the environmental conditions have allowed black-box firms to grow into one of the largest sources of liquidity in the marketplace.

Although unbundling and best-execution mandates were not intended to benefit the black-box community, these regulatory reforms adversely affected the informational advantages once held by their largest competitors; market makers at investment banks. The erosion of execution consolidation created opportunities for new entrants to compete with traditional liquidity providers.

In a similar light, the growth of order segmentation practices by asset managers furthered the industry's investment in technology infrastructure for low-touch execution platforms. Black-box firms gained from the stability and breadth of the offers that investment banks were building for their traditional client base.

An industry in which liquidity was once negotiated over the phone has now evolved into an array of execution venues. Black-box strategies have become one of the most predominant sources of liquidity. Statistical arbitrage, market-neutral strategies, and AMM each have unique ways of providing liquidity to the marketplace and improving the interactions between buy-and-hold investors.

Investor assets clearly remain dominated within the institutional investors of traditional mutual and pension funds, although hedge funds have grown into a $1.2 trillion-dollar industry. Their assets, however, are still dwarfed by the assets of traditional investment managers, which are estimated to be a $17 trillion-dollar industry (see figure 9.5).

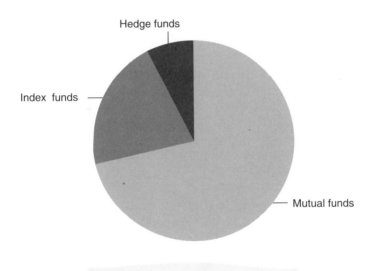

**FIGURE 9.5**    Assets by investment strategy

The assets of hedge funds are not indicative of their relative activity level in the market. A traditional asset manager has multiyear investment horizons, so the turnover ratio of its portfolio is often less than 1×. If it has $1 billion in assets under management, its trading activity over the course of the year is less than $1 billion. Hedge funds on the other hand have turnover ratios of 4× to 5× of their assets, reflecting their short investment horizon and their usage of leverage to increase returns. Black-box firms are off the charts, trading 20× to 50× of their assets annually. The ecology of the market liquidity is disproportional to the assets top institutional holders as a result.

Investors are provided transparency on the major institutional and private holdings of stocks. Any retail investor keen to know who are the largest shareholders of Google, Starbucks, or Procter & Gamble may simply view the holdings reports available on the Yahoo! Finance website. In the most liquid S&P 500 stocks, the holdings reports will often have the same firms as top-10 holders, reflecting the concentration of assets with the traditional investment managers.

Investors are provided with few metrics, however, on the demographics of the daily turnover in the stockmarket. Are we to assume the most active transactions in Google are in line with the largest shareholders? Or do market speculators command a much larger share of the market gyrations?

Liquidity is not what it used to be in any case. Black-box strategies have grown to be in excess of 30 percent of every market transaction. The gap between the holders and traders of stocks has never been so disproportional (see figure 9.6).

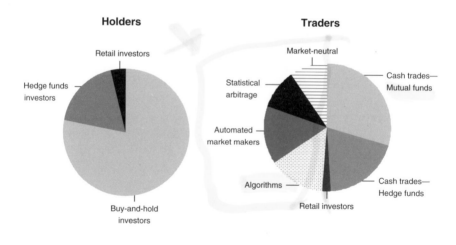

**FIGURE 9.6**   Ecology of the marketplace

The buy-and-hold investor is no less significant; it just has a different role and a new set of counterparts when seeking liquidity. How the evolution of the ecology of the marketplace influences the relationship between price and value can only be answered in time. One thing is certain: the most active investors today are computers.

# CHAPTER 10

# Globalization of Equity Markets

## *Why Does American Airlines Have a Higher Trading Volume than Singapore Airlines?*

S ingapore Airlines is one of the most recognized corporate brands in the airline industry. For both the general public and business travelers, Singapore Airlines has established a reputation as the best in class for air travel. The firm has had a leadership role in transforming the airline industry, from pioneering individual TV screens throughout economy class to letting passengers print their boarding passes at home and avoid check-in queues.

Singapore Airlines has correspondingly been one of the most profitable airlines in the industry over the past two decades. Given the stellar reputation for quality, customers have been more than willing to pay a premium to fly on their planes. First-class passengers in particular have been willing to pay for the luxury of private suites, designed by the French fashion house Givenchy.

In the 2008 *Wall Street Journal Asia 200* survey conducted by the market research firm Colmar Brunton, Singapore Airlines ranked #1 in management vision, quality of service, and corporate reputation.[1] It was the only firm to hold the top spot in the survey without interruption since 1993. For these reasons, the island-state's most prominent company has grown into the world's biggest airline by market value.

Despite the success story of Singapore Airlines, the company's stock, listed on the Singapore Stock Exchange, only commands $20–$30 million dollars a day of turnover. That's roughly 50–60 percent of American Airlines, a company that has been through several rounds of bankruptcy protection in the past two decades and has a market capitalization of less than 10 percent of Singapore Airlines capitalization. Singapore Airlines is certainly an attractive stock to own, so why is there such a large gap in trading volume from its industry peers?

The disparity in turnover levels is in part a representation of the "velocity" of the marketplace. The velocity of turnover is simply a measure of the value traded relative to the market capitalization. Velocity ranks the frequency that the total shares outstanding are exchanged among investors.

A small-capitalization stock with a valuation of $700 million and annual turnover of $350 million is said to have a velocity of 50 percent because half its market capitalization trades each year. Stocks with higher velocity metrics are more heavily speculated in than their peers, presumably because of changing hands more often (see table 10.1).

**Table 10.1**   Top-10 markets ranked by velocity

| Market | Velocity of turnover |
| --- | --- |
| Nasdaq | 811% |
| China–Shenzhen | 285% |
| American (AMEX) | 279% |
| Germany | 236% |
| New York (NYSE) | 205% |
| Italy | 198% |
| Korea | 189% |
| Spain | 179% |
| Taiwan | 155% |
| London | 155% |

*Source:* World Federation of Exchanges

The Nasdaq market has a higher velocity metric than any other global marketplace, by a long margin. The Nasdaq's velocity of 811 percent represents that each listed security trades 8× its market capitalization each year. Of the remaining top-10 most active markets, their velocity metrics are 2× market capitalization.

The NYSE, where American Airlines is listed, has a velocity of 205 percent, almost 3× the velocity of the Singapore Stock Exchange. There are several explanations for U.S. markets having such prominent activity levels compared to global exchanges. The liquidity is a function of the size of the U.S. economy, the strength of the financial and regulatory environment, and the sophistication of the investor base, both domestic and foreigners.

Velocity of the marketplace is influenced by economics, investor sentiment, technology, market mechanisms and rules, costs of trading, taxes, and regulatory environment. Why Singapore Airlines trades a

fraction of American Airlines has less to do with the attractive
the company's fundamentals, and more to do with the attractiveness
of the exchange where it's traded.

Black-box firms, too, are large contributors to the velocity of the
marketplace. Statistical arbitrage, market-neutral investing, AMM, and
algos have been very much a U.S.-centric story over the past decade.
As black-box firms have embraced "globalization" of their trading
models, they have been one of the biggest contributors of volume
expansion in global markets.

Volume expansion is arguably one of the most significant influences
on global equity markets because it increases the prominence of the
financial industry, but also stresses the market structure to accommo-
date growth. Volume expansion places pressure on brokers, exchanges,
and regulators to improve the efficiency of their execution process and
to reduce their costs of trading.

Black-box strategies, unlike any other investment strategy, cast a big
footprint in the markets where they feed. When they adapt their trading
models to international markets, they receive significant attention from
the local financial community; sometimes favorable, sometimes less so.

## GLOBALIZATION OF TRADING STRATEGIES

Globalization, in the economic sense, is the integration of national
economies through increased trade, foreign investment, capital flows,
and liberalization of policy. Modern globalization has been an iterative
process since World War II, and many economists would argue that the
pace of globalization has quickened in the past decade through greater
international trade, advancements in technology, and outsourcing. The
world is flatter than ever before.

The globalization of investing has correspondingly quickened in
recent years, highlighted by the capital inflows into emerging markets, such as China and India. Over the past 50 years, barriers to
international investment have crumbled among emerging economies,
allowing investors to purchase securities in many foreign markets with
few restrictions. Technology has played an important role in the liber-
ation of international investing, through reducing the costs of trading
and the flow of information.

Advancements in electronic trading technology have rapidly accelerated the globalization of equity markets, in the sense that an investor
based in Santa Fe can transact in securities from Japan to Portugal in

a seamless way. Technology has facilitated access to a wide range of equity markets and it has encapsulated the unique differences between countries. In the past decade, quantitative investors have embarked on globalization too, albeit they have often encountered unique challenges compared to traditional investors.

Traditional investors, who have a long-term view on a market or region, are not time sensitive to implementation of their investment strategies, nor are they sensitive to frictional costs. They can afford to be patient with their investment strategies. If a mutual fund desires a strategy in an emerging market, such as Portugal, its main constraint is raising capital with its domestic audience. There are few, if any, constraints on its ability to implement its strategies in emerging markets. Foreign investor limitations, perhaps, but most markets are accommodating to foreign firms.

Black-box firms, by contrast, face unique constraints when porting their strategies from region to region. Their strategies are impeded by differing costs of execution, market rules, market mechanisms, and investor behavior. Quantitative traders need to learn to navigate the local market structure to implement their investment strategies.

As black-box traders have embraced "globalization," they have learned much about the differences in market structure around the globe. One of the greatest differences in global equity markets is the technology gap between the U.S. markets and the other major global exchanges. While the U.S. markets handle upward of several hundred millions of transactions per day, some of the largest global markets can handle only a fraction of the U.S. capacity.

## The Technology Gap

In January 2006, the TSE was facing unprecedented volume growth. The euphoria surrounding China's emergence on the global stage had renewed the appetites of the global investment managers in Japanese opportunities. Japan was once again attracting massive amounts of foreign capital, largely on the back of its increasing trading relationship with China, which had grown from 30 percent to 70 percent of Japan's gross domestic product in the previous decade.

Japan had always been one of the most active global marketplaces. Even throughout the pessimistic period of its "Lost Decade" of stagnant economic growth, the daily turnover on the TSE was still in the range of $10 billion–$15 billion a day, the world's second-most active exchange in dollar volume.

In the fourth quarter of 2005, trading volumes on the TSE would approach $25 billion per day, nearing the peaks observed during the 1980s heydays. Mutual funds, pension funds, and hedge funds had all been allocating assets to Asia, and Japan's volume growth was an illustration of the investor excitement in the region. The TSE would finish the year with a 40 percent gain in 2005, reflecting the renewed appetites of foreign investors.

Japanese investors, however, would soon begin to revisit fears of an overvalued equity market. Following their return from the New Year *shogatsu* holiday, Japanese investors would ponder the impact of a variety of negative earnings reports. The U.S. technology bellwethers, Intel and Yahoo!, had reported worse-than-expected fourth-quarter earnings results. The U.S. technology sector would be downgraded in the first week of 2006, and investors began to speculate that the Japanese blue chips, such as Softbank, Toshiba, Canon, and Sony Corp., would also post disappointing earnings.

More bad news arrived. On January 18, 2006, Japanese newspapers reported an investigation had begun into Livedoor's CEO Yomiuri Shimbun for allegedly concealing a ¥1 billion deficit in previous earnings. Shimbun was a popular technology entrepreneur. He was an unconventional executive in Japan, sporting t-shirts and jeans, and he had risen to celebrity status. The breakout of the scandal became known as the "Livedoor Shock."[2]

Panic selling in Japan's largest technology stocks would ensue. The combination of poor U.S. earnings and a local scandal were sufficient catalysts to push the Nikkei downward 6 percent in just two days. Investors would learn there was more to worry about in the coming days.

The TSE was nearing its capacity. Although the value of trading was below previous peaks of $25 billion, the numbers of individual transactions occurring on the TSE were approaching all-time highs. The TSE was having difficulty processing all the transactions. Investors were experiencing greater and greater latency throughout the trading session. The TSE's servers just weren't designed for the high numbers of transactions.

On January 18, the number of transactions approached 3.5 million, which sparked the TSE into taking preventive actions. During the lunch session, the TSE officials would make an impromptu announcement: the TSE would be closing 20 minutes early.

To manage the rapid volume expansion, the TSE would close early to prevent the number of transactions from breaching capacity, estimated to be about four million trades per day. Not only did investors have poor earnings and a Livedoor scandal on their plate, but also they had technology to be concerned with. What if the TSE was to close the session before they could sell? It was a further catalyst to increase their aggressive selling around the next day's market open.

Trading activity on January 19 would approach two million transactions just one hour into the morning session. Although trading activity subsided by the lunch session, the TSE took no chances. It made a formal decision to remove 30 minutes from their afternoon session until further notice. By removing 30 minutes from its four-hour trading session, it was estimating that it would reduce market volume by 25 percent or 500,000 trades.

The reduced market hours would remain in place for the coming weeks as the TSE implemented upgrades to its technology. Its novel approach proved to be successful because the TSE did not breach its capacity throughout the period of rapid volume expansion. The Livedoor Shock became more renowned for exposing the legacy technology issues of the TSE than the scandal of Shimbun.

In hindsight, the TSE cannot be blamed for lack of foresight on the impact of volume expansion. Throughout its Lost Decade, the priority of banking regulatory reforms obviously outweighed the sentiments on investment in trading technology. There's little need to improve the frequency of investor order flows if there are no reasons to invest.

The Livedoor Shock exemplified the technology gap between Japan and the U.S. markets. While Nasdaq investors have become accustomed to transacting in billions of orders a day, Japanese investors were limited to a fraction of the U.S. capacity. Although globalization has quickened the process of international trade, black-box firms have been learning that the gaps around the global equity markets are often very pronounced. Some strategies are easily ported from one region to another; while other strategies are unsupportive based on differences in the market structure.

## THE GLOBAL LANDSCAPE

Although there have been pockets of technical trading in all corners of the world, the U.S. has clearly led the proliferation of black-box trading. The U.S. financial system has always been at the forefront of innovation to sustain the world's largest economy. Advancements in technology and an environment of competition have created the ideal playground for quantitative investment strategies in the U.S. markets.

On a global perspective, the integration of world economics has created stronger relationships between markets and corporations. The prosperity of any particular country is a function of the health of the world economy as a whole. Global stock markets are more strongly correlated than ever before. Quantitative traders, however, face many barriers in capturing those relationships given the vast differences in market structure.

The gap in quantitative trading opportunities is best highlighted in the transactional activity in American stock markets relative to the rest of the world. In 2008, the U.S. marketplace averaged $277 billion of daily transactions, roughly 65 percent of the world's total market activity of $432 billion a day (see figure 10.1). The prominence of U.S. activity, although it cannot be attributed to any particular factor, reflects the success of the market structures that sustain such a high capacity of diverse investors.

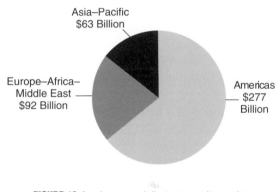

**FIGURE 10.1**  Average daily turnover by region
*Source:* World Federation of Exchanges

Quantitative investment strategies are largely governed by the liquidity of the marketplace. Unlike traditional investment funds, which may impose constraints around market capitalization, quantitative trading strategies are typically constrained by liquidity. High-frequency traders take small bets across thousands of securities, with firms constraining their strategies to a few percent of the daily volume, rather than building concentrated positions that would be held for the long term.

From the vantage of liquidity, the U.S. markets clearly have offered the best opportunities for quantitative investors, given the breadth and depth of the marketplace. Daily volumes of $277 billion across thousands of securities create an environment with opportunities for momentum trading, market-neutral, or market-making strategies (see figure 10.2). The U.S. markets, however, reflect a degree of saturation. There are obviously many players chasing the same signals.

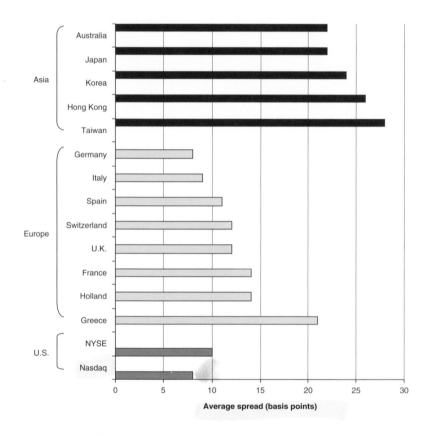

**FIGURE 10.2**  Average daily turnover of major global markets
*Source:* World Federation of Exchanges

It's difficult to estimate the total percentage of black-box traders in the U.S. markets. No industry watchdog monitors the demographics of participants or the trading frequency of investors. Whether the average holding period is 18 months or 18 minutes is difficult to reverse engineer in the aftermath of the day's transactional records.

## European Markets

The opportunities for black-box trading on a global perspective are different than those in the U.S. markets. They vary in each region because of liquidity, market structure, costs of trading, volatility, and the regulatory framework. There are 23 global markets with in excess of a $1 billion of volume a day.

The LSE is the most active exchange in Europe with in excess of $25 billion of volume a day. Across Europe, market liquidity is concentrated in a few financial centers. Almost 70 percent of Europe's total daily volume occurs in London, Germany, Spain, and Italy.

Quantitative models that depend on hedging long/short positions across countries and sectors must overcome the challenge of accessing liquidity across a fragmented region. There are 14 major markets in Europe, spanning three time zones. The "pan-European" trading session is a 12-hour day, with staggered market opens, lunch sessions, and windows of liquidity.

Unlike the U.S. markets, Europe doesn't have the advantage of a single market with a deep pool of liquidity. Trading a single sector, such as financial stocks, would necessitate transacting across a dozen markets, navigating the different regulatory requirements and market mechanisms.

Europe's adoption of the MiFID in 2007 could be the major catalyst for the consolidation of liquidity, similar to the U.S. markets.

## Asian Markets

In Asia, black-box trading has largely been a Japan story. Japan liberalized its markets in the 1980s, relaxing foreign restrictions and local tariffs. All varieties of quantitative trading are sustainable in Japan's $20 billion marketplace, albeit the technology platforms of the TSE constrains the ultra-high-frequency opportunities that have materialized in the U.S. markets.

There have been many suggestions that the "pan-Asia" marketplace is evolving along the same lines as Europe, but there are vast differences in geography, culture, economics, and politics to limit the chances of an integrated financial center. Even defining a boundary to the Asia marketplace is a challenge. There are 12 major markets, spanning four time zones and representing eight national languages, let alone countless dialects. Unlike in Europe, where day trips including four countries are feasible, in Asia a trip to Mumbai, Tokyo, and Sydney would represent a 24-hour commute.

Tokyo, Hong Kong, and Singapore have established strong regional hedge fund communities. Each region has its merits for trading the entire region, albeit there are many liabilities to centralize trading in one city hub. Hong Kong is conveniently located for China and North Asia, but it's less well suited for India. Singapore has become the epicenter for the Association of South East Asian Nations and India, but it's an eight-hour flight from Japan.

The diverse regulatory environment distinguishes the Asian marketplace further from Europe. The two most prominent emerging markets, China and India, both impose a Qualified Foreign Investors, which constrains foreign investors. Korea and Taiwan similarly maintain restrictions on foreign investors, constraining most U.S. firms to execute with structured asset products (i.e. equity swaps).

Electronic trading, the infrastructure to sustain quantitative trading, is only permitted without restrictions in Japan, Australia, Hong Kong, and Singapore. In 2008, a survey by Greenwich Associates estimated that the Asia–Pacific markets had less than 5 percent electronic trading clients.

Technology, regulations, and friction costs of trading, such as local-country stamp taxes, have been inhibitors of quantitative firms porting their strategies to Asia. With the exception of Japan, the Asian marketplace is highly fragmented. Despite a dozen major markets, the liquidity is concentrated in about 700 to 800 securities, and fewer than half of those stocks can be traded electronically without restrictions.

Despite the euphoria surrounding China and India's entrance to the world stage, the elimination of barriers to accessing most of Asia's markets is a work in progress.

## DIVERSITY OF EQUITY MICROSTRUCTURE

The globalization of equity markets was accelerated by the advancements in technology and electronic trading infrastructure. With DMA, investors could transact in equity markets from almost any corner of the globe, receiving live price quotes and real-time execution. Black-box investors have been at the forefront of the globalization process, connecting to every market that has become available in the electronic revolution.

Even if a strategy is designed on a common technical indicator, the "same signal" may be transacted differently in each region because of market structure. The models themselves typically need to be calibrated (or optimized) to fit the uniqueness of each market.[3]

The quantitative funds that have been successful in globalization are the ones to have successfully navigated the local market structure, learning the nuances of the market mechanisms and understanding the determinants of their strategy margins. They have learned that the global marketplace is anything but apples-to-apples for black-box strategies in one region to the next.

## Costs of Trading

Execution costs are one of the largest determinants of the feasibility of high-frequency trading. As the costs of execution increase, the constraints on the frequency of trading increase. More expensive markets will result in strategies with longer holding periods because the strategies must yield a higher profit to overcome the frictional effects. The fixed costs of execution alone can greatly vary from region to region because of differences in settlement fee structures, local taxes, and brokerage commission rates.

The U.S. markets have the lowest cost structure in the world, with execution fees of less than one cent per trade. Most global markets have not achieved the economies of scale to compare with the U.S. markets' competitiveness. Emerging markets, in particular, may have brokerage commissions that are 20 times higher than those of the U.S. markets.

The variable costs of execution, such as market impact costs, vary greatly from region to region because of liquidity, average spreads, and volatility. The average bid–offer spread remains one of the largest determinants of impact costs. Spreads vary greatly across global markets, in part as a reflection of the underlying fixed costs, such as taxes and settlement fees, that market makers bear, but also spreads vary because of market mechanisms, such as minimum tick sizes, as discussed earlier (see figure 10.3).

On a global perspective, average spreads vary from less than 10 basis points to in excess of 30 basis points in the most liquid foreign markets. Correspondingly, the variable costs of trading differ greatly around the globe. The spread can become the greatest influence on trading costs given that brokerage commissions have gravitated toward single digits of basis points.

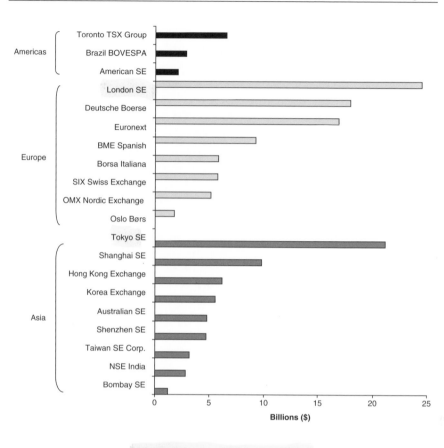

**FIGURE 10.3** Average daily turnover

Although it may be advantageous for an exchange to lower its minimum tick size to that of global markets, the decision is rarely that simple. The capacity of the exchange, the settlement procedures, and sentiments from the local brokerage community all play a role. The difference in spreads is only one example of how the global markets are at different phases of their evolution.

The market mechanisms can vary greatly from region to region. Some exchanges have open auctions while others have a closed auction. Some accept market orders while others limit orders. Some have lunch breaks while others are open 24 hours a day. Although electronic trading products encapsulate some of the unique differences in market mechanisms, how investors must access liquidity varies greatly from region to region.

## Market Access

Regulations are arguably the most diverse aspect of global investment. Each region adopts best practices for their local financial community and for the prevailing economic climate. Despite an appreciation for global integration, the world remains one of differing priorities and solutions for the same objectives.

Short-sell executions are case in point of the diversity of market regulations. Despite short-sell rules being one of the more sensitive areas of financial regulations, there are few standards around their implementation (see table 10.2).

**Table 10.2**  Short-sell price restrictions

| | U.S. | London | Japan | Hong Kong | Taiwan |
|---|---|---|---|---|---|
| **Price restriction on short sale** | No short sale on an uptick. | No short sale on an uptick. | A short-sell transaction should not be executed at a price less than the latest announced execution price. | A short-sell order must be executed at the best current ask price. | A short sale must not be lower than the previous closing price. |

The differing usage of language to describe a similar concept is a striking example of the differences in regulatory regimes. Short-sell regulations are further convoluted by restrictions on stock borrowing, order-handling requirements, documentation, and so on.

Academics and investors would concur that there is no single market structure that represents the paradigm for others to emulate. Each market imposes regulations to prioritize the needs of its financial community and economic climate. How this applies to black-box trading is that some strategies are well suited in one region, and less suited for another.

The "same signal" will be chased differently in markets around the globe. A statistical arbitrage strategy that may have generated $10 billion of annual turnover across a thousand stocks might only generate $30 million across 50 stocks when implemented in Taiwan. The average holding periods of market-neutral strategies might be a few days in an NYSE strategy, but may average three weeks when implemented on the French Bourse.

Each market improvement and liberalization represents a potential opportunity for the proliferation of black-box strategies, but also quantitative investors must be cognizant of the adverse reforms as they embark on their journey of globalization.

## REGULATORY RISK

Whether the global markets evolve to achieve the levels of U.S. market velocity is uncertain. Market volume, just like prices, can go either way. The influence of black-box investment strategies, in particular, is not well understood by the financial community. The biggest concern for black-box firms is the regulatory risk of protectionist policies. Unlike other types of investors, regulatory reforms can eliminate their strategies outright.

Financial crises have a particular way of igniting regulatory reforms. In the postmortem of every major financial crisis, the role of market participants has been questioned with respect to their contribution to the economic instability. Black-box firms can be disadvantaged by the changing tide of regulatory reforms. A financial crisis gives industry watchdogs the atmosphere to introduce measures that, presumably, will prevent recurrences of subsequent economic instability.

In an article by legal professor Larry Ribstein entitled "The Bubble Laws," he described this recurring pattern in financial history as a "boom–bubble–bust–regulate" cycle.[5] A boom encourages trust in the markets, leading to speculation and risk taking, and ultimately an overvalued market bubble. When the bust occurs, it's usually followed by an equally speculative frenzy of regulation. As Ribstein comments, the atmosphere following a crisis is not conducive to thoughtful policymaking.

The 1997 Asian Currency Crisis was a financial crisis that inspired a wave of regulatory reforms that affected an entire region. The Asian Currency Crisis began in Thailand in May 1997 when hedge funds began a speculative attack to sell Thailand's currency, the baht, short in belief that the Thai government would be unable to defend the currency's fixed rate to the U.S. dollar.

After a period of defending the fixed rate, the Thai government would eventually succumb to speculators and allow a free float of the currency in the public markets. The hedge funds were successful in their attack on the currency because the baht would decline 40 percent in a matter of days. Thailand's booming economy would go into a tailspin, with firms suffering massive layoffs and investors suffering asset price devaluations.

In the coming weeks, the crisis spread across most of Southeast Asia and Japan and would devalue stock markets and property assets. Hedge funds would continue with speculative attacks on other regional currencies by massively short selling the Malaysian ringgit, Indonesian rupiah, South Korean won, and Hong Kong dollar. Governments were spending billions of their foreign reserves to defend their currency valuations.

The crisis would leave significant macroeconomic effects, inclusive of sharp devaluations in the currencies and stock markets. The nominal gross domestic product of the region would fall by double digits across most countries. Political upheaval would be an outcome with the resignation of Indonesia's President Suharto and Thailand's Prime Minister General Chavalit Yongchaiyudh. The crisis would also ignite significant anti-Western sentiments, with U.S. hedge funds singled out.

The government of Malaysia announced the most radical measures to regulate the trade in its local currency, the ringgit, and to reduce the country's exposure to financial speculators. In September 1997, it would announce that the ringgit would be fixed to the U.S. dollar and it would be tradable only within Malaysia. The capital measures would inhibit the currency from entering and leaving the country.

Malaysian Prime Minister Dr Mahathir bin Mohamad accused George Soros of ruining Malaysia's economy with massive currency speculation.[6] In his words:

> It [the crisis] has destroyed the hard work of countries in order to cater to the interests of speculators—as if their interests are so important that millions of people must suffer.

The regulatory reforms enacted during the Asian Crisis would not be shortlived constraints. In the postmortem of the crisis, the Southeast Asian governments would dramatically alter their treatment of foreign investors, with a particular emphasis on constraining the outflows of capital. Many of the protectionist reforms remain in place today throughout Southeast Asia.

The 2008 global financial tsunami will likely see a variety of market reforms targeted against speculative activities. Black-box traders will likely be found in the crossfire of regulatory constraints because the role of their investment activities in the marketplace is often misunderstood. "Regulatory risk" consequently remains the greatest concern for the proliferation of their investment philosophy.

Any change in market structure can result in unintended consequences to the marketplace, perhaps even eliminating particular types of investment strategies. Short-sell restrictions, capital gains taxes, and minimum holding periods are only a few of the many suggestions put forth to ringfence Wall Street's culture of risk taking.

In February 2009, Congressman Peter DeFazio introduced House Resolution 1068, which seeks to impose a 0.25 percent tax on all security transactions.[7] DeFazio's inspiration for this "trader tax" is to force Wall Street to pay for the Troubled Asset Relief Program with transaction taxes. In his view, this tax would raise money from Wall Street with negligible impact on the average investor.

Although the retail investors may not be adversely affected by taxes on a few transactions each month, the trader tax could introduce costs of another nature. A transactional tax of 0.25 percent could all but eliminate the margins of high-frequency traders, from statistical arbitrage to AMM.

What would be the impact to the market's volume if there were no black-box strategies? Would a transaction tax increase the average bid–offer spreads in U.S. securities to their 1990s levels of 30 basis points? Would market turnover decline by 10 percent, 30 percent, 50 percent, or more? The "costs" borne by the average investor could not be approximated by the taxation of 0.25 percent alone.

In part, the root of the problem resides in the image of the black-box industry. What is the influence of its trading on the global markets? Despite the empirical evidence that its strategies offer a dampening effect on market volatility and lower bid–offer spreads, there is no conclusive evidence on the role black-box strategies play in the financial markets.

Arguably the largest contributors to volume expansion in the past decade have been the proliferating black-box investment firms. Their volume, however, is not always welcome. When you cast a large footprint, you're bound to step on a few toes.

# CHAPTER 11

# An Adaptive Industry

## *What Signals Will They Be Chasing Next?*

S uccessful quantitative firms are not simply founded on their knowledge of mathematics and physics. They are equally founded on the
innovation and creativity of their people. Longevity, for a black-box
firm, is rooted in its ability to extract the best ideas from their people
and to continuously adapt to an increasingly competitive market place.

Perhaps more so than any other investment strategy, black-box
trading is subject to tough economic challenges. They find that main-
taining an edge on execution is an ongoing arms race of technology.
They experience that subtle changes in the regulatory environment can
dramatically alter the profit opportunities of their models. They learn
of competitors, targeting similar price anomalies and crowding their
margins.

The longevity of black-box strategies is unlike that of any other
investment strategy as well. They prosper in unique economic conditions, defined by volatility, dispersion, serial correlation, or spreads.
Their businesses do not benefit from the overall prosperity of the
economy, when the rising tide lifts all boats.

As David Kabiller, one of the founding partners of AQR Capital,
described it:[1]

> You sow the seeds of your own destruction by too many people embrac-
> ing it—that's why we think that a lot of the best strategies out there have
> finite capacity to them, because the more money that's attracted to them,
> the more likely that over time they'll be degraded.

The survival of a quantitative firm is consequently a function of
the quality of its research process, of its ability to execute its research
models, and of its instincts about the changing landscape of the financial
markets. The strategies' success story has been more than a story about
what signals they chase; it's also a story about how they chase them.

**163**

# THE DECAY EFFECT

There was no greater example of finite capacity than that which was experienced during the first week of August 2007. It was a unique moment in the history of quantitative trading, where the financial community became painfully aware of just how many black-box firms were embracing the same strategy.

In a research paper "What Happened to the Quants in August 2007?," Andrew Lo and Amir Khandani presented a plausible explanation for the market turmoil experienced by the quantitative hedge funds.[2] They hypothesized that hedge funds had experienced a decay effect of a particular statistical arbitrage strategy known as the "contrarian" strategy.

In this particular contrarian strategy, black-box firms attempt to profit on a short-term (as in one day) price discrepancy that materializes around market overreactions. The assumption is that investors often buy (or sell) too aggressively, and the market reverts to its previous level when their trading is finished. A contrarian investor can profit on this pattern by buying all the losers and selling all the winners, at the end of every trading day.

In its simplest form, a contrarian strategy would buy yesterday's losers and sell yesterday's winners, and then profit on the reversal that occurs the next day. Lo and Khandani simulated the trading profits from this strategy in U.S. equities from 1995 to 2007 and highlighted how lucrative this strategy would have been (at least on paper). In 1995, the strategy produced an annualized return of 345 percent.

Their results were overly optimistic, as the author highlights, for several reasons: transaction costs, short-sell restrictions, technology constraints to name a few. Their backtest simulation assumed that more than 4,500 stocks would be traded each day, which wouldn't have been feasible in 1995, nor today by even the most technology-savvy firms. Nevertheless, their research proved there were substantial excess returns for the firms that could implement a variation of the strategy.

The series of events that led to the turmoil of August 2007 arguably would had begun in the early 1990s when initial research into contrarian investing was first published. The price anomaly is known as "cross-autocorrelation," in which stock returns are negatively correlated from one day to the next.

In quantitative finance, the industry is one of shared ideas because academics will publish studies of price anomalies and will circulate them among the investment community. The interesting ideas, such as contrarian trading, will get digested throughout the industry and will get implemented by many different firms, although in slightly differentiated forms.

In the mid-1990s, the proprietary desks at investments banks would have been the few financial institutions that could have capitalized on this contrarian price anomaly. They had the benefit of technology connectivity to the exchange's electronic order books (i.e. SuperDot), years before this infrastructure was available to hedge funds. But also, proprietary desks had a huge advantage in that they didn't have to pay for trading commissions. This gave them a leg-up in pursuing high-turnover strategies, at a time when trading commissions were as much as 0.50 percent per transaction.

In the late 1990s, when electronic trading technology became available, hedge fund entrants would have began to exploit the contrarian strategy. Certainly there were ample hedge funds to have been chasing this discrepancy. Their early attempts may have been for holding periods of longer than a day, but as commissions decreased in the subsequent years, their trading would have migrated toward higher frequency of turnover and begun to resemble that of their competitors at proprietary trading desks.

As Lo and Khandani suggest, the effects of many firms employing a similar strategy were observed in the "decay" of the strategy. They demonstrate in their simulation that the average daily returns of the contrarian strategy declined from 1.38 percent in 1995 to 0.13 percent by 2007 (see figure 11.1). The profit margins decayed to a fraction of their original levels because so many firms were *chasing the same signals.*

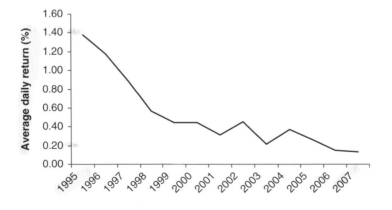

**FIGURE 11.1**   Decay of contrarian strategy

The contrarian traders had effectively simulated the role of a liquidity provider. By buying losers and selling winners, contrarians were adding to the demand for out-of-flavor stocks and increasing the supply of fashionable stocks, thereby stabilizing the supply and demand imbalances. Hedge funds were adding enormous amounts of liquidity to the market because they were using technology and applying optimized models to contrarian trading. The effects were that they were reducing market volatility and were dampening the market movements away from the index.

The other effect, however, was that they were cannibalizing each other's profits. The strategy decay forced these firms to engage in leverage to sustain their profits. By using leverage, they could increase the magnitude of their portfolio and amplify the returns of their strategy, in line with the previous years of returns.

As the research of Lo and Khandani suggests, the contrarian strategy would have required multiples of leverage in 2007 to achieve the same performance of just a few years earlier in 2001. A hedge fund with $1 billion of assets employing this strategy would have been trading like a $5 billion fund.

The effects of the synchronous unwind were felt during the first week of August 2007. The contrarians sent the equity markets into a tailspin as they simultaneously headed for the exits. One firm, by conventional wisdom, cannot move the market; several firms, holding similar positions, with similar risk preferences can clearly create a short-term impact.

Although the events of August 2007 didn't leave a lasting impact on the valuation of the markets, they did leave a lasting impression on the financial community. Black-box firms, despite being a niche community in the financial industry, certainly had grown to represent a significant influence on the stock markets from Wall Street to Shanghai.

## THE SEARCH FOR SIGNALS

The decay effect of quantitative strategies is even further exasperated by another unique dilemma: finite data resources. Signals are limited by what can and cannot be measured. And once a data source develops a reputation in the community, it becomes widely demanded and widely available.

Some of the earliest entrants into quantitative trading in the 1980s began their careers as commodity trading advisors, who each day typed price quotes into Lotus 123 spreadsheets. Their initial success spawned an industry of data vendors, which commercialized the capture of time-series data and sold it throughout the financial community. Thomson Reuters, the industry's leading vendor of financial information, now offers depths of 15+ years history for almost every stock market transaction. Emerging markets like Mauritius may be scare, but otherwise 90 percent of the world's transactions are archived in a database.

Fundamental stock data have also matured. Balance-sheet metrics, macroeconomic data, corporate actions, historical archives, and so on are now widely available for purchase. Even if a black-box firm is a first mover to use a historical data set, it will have difficulty maintaining an edge based on a particular source of data alone.

Similarly, there are fewer opportunities to differentiate strategies when constrained by the same, widely available information. As the saying goes, "there are only so many ways to skin a cat." Mathematicians, physicists, and economists have manipulated market quotes of open, high, low, and close price data for the past two decades. Engineering better models based on the same resources is an unrealistic undertaking.

Signals are a peculiar animal, however. A signal doesn't become a signal by chance. It takes an economist, scientist, or entrepreneur to unlock the value of an emerging data source before it truly becomes known as a source of signals. The commercial value of discovering new signals, whether in business, science, or finance, has led to several instances of discovery for new and innovative data sources.

## Weather Data

In 1999, a new flavor of scientists arrived on Wall Street: meteorologists were being employed by hedge funds and investment banks to develop in-house proprietary models for forecasting weather patterns. For obvious reasons, many industries such as agriculture, airlines, or tourism are affected by seasonal trends in the weather. Wall Street realized that external sources of weather analysis were not differentiated and it felt it could earn profits with a more refined forecast.[3]

There were many areas for hedge funds to exploit weather research. In 1999, the Chicago Mercantile Exchange (CME) had just begun listing weather derivative contracts such as "temperature index derivatives," which were derived on the actual recorded temperatures in major

U.S. cities. Temperature index derivatives are based on a calculation of daily temperature from a baseline; for instance, each degree below 65 Fahrenheit counts as one "heating degree day" (HDD). The HDD total over a period quantifies the aggregate temperature observed.

Temperature index futures were beneficial as hedging mechanisms for industries sensitive to unseasonable weather. Ski resorts could use the derivatives to offset the risk of a warm winter. Farmers could offset their risk of a particularly rainy summer. Hedge funds, correspondingly, could earn profits with an accurate model of weather forecasts.

Meteorologists were employed on Wall Street to study weather patterns. Similar to traditional equity research based on earnings projections, meteorologists would develop models around rainfall, wind speed, and cloud cover. They would study the historical relationships of these variables and would devise more precise measurements than those available at external news agencies.

Hedge funds were willing to invest in the state-of-the-art infrastructure necessary to commercialize the analysis of weather data, just as they were willing to expense their analysis of Nasdaq order books. Some of the top-tier multistrategy hedge funds—D.E. Shaw & Co., Tudor Investments, Susquehanna—paired statisticians with seasoned meteorologists to devise novel ways of exploiting weather forecasts. They created databases of weather patterns from hundreds of U.S. cities dating back decades and then began to quantify the correlation of weather metrics.

Their research led to innovative new strategies of "relative value" weather models. If their models were showing that airstreams were stronger in one region, they could look for a correlated market to hedge the uncertainty. They could buy Baltimore weather derivatives and hedge with Philadelphia, where the weather is normally related. By investing in weather research, quantitative firms were able to exploit an information advantage over the investment community.

In less than a decade from the CME's debut of weather derivatives, an entire industry of hedge fund strategies had evolved around this chaotic underlying phenomena. With the breadth of technology applied to monitoring global warming, such as satellite imagery, underwater seismic systems, and micro-weather balloons, black-box firms are likely to uncover more innovative "signals" in the future. And the National Weather Service should expect that many of their alumni will continue to join the ranks of the highest-paid analysts on Wall Street.

## Location Data

The next time you glance at your BlackBerry, it might be intriguing to know you're signaling the next generation of black-box strategies with important information. A Friday night out at the movies followed by martinis in a trendy nightclub district just might ignite a wave of buying in the consumer goods sector when the markets open come Monday.

Why scientists and entrepreneurs are excited about location data was highlighted in a *Newsweek* article entitled "A Trillion Points of Data."[4] A mobile phone is a kind of sensor. Every time that you make a call or download information, you are communicating your location to your cellular network provider. Billions of mobile phones translate into a massive database of location information for scientists and business executives to study the relationship of location and economic activity.

Businesses have an inherent need to understand their customers. An unanticipated change in consumer preferences can be very costly if a business has made the wrong investments in inventory. Survey firms and management consultants advise the private sector in this regard, but so often they can only provide crude analysis. Location information potentially will bring a real-time window into specific customer trends. Whether it's where Florida teenagers are choosing to dine or where midwestern seniors have recently been shopping, location data can provide timely insights on specific demographic trends.

Although the application of location data is in its infancy, hedge funds have already begun to explore the statistical significance of location patterns to movements in the S&P 500. Does an increase in traffic congestion signal a pending increase in the price of oil is the concern for the next generation of black-box strategies. And your BlackBerry may become the next signal their strategies are chasing.

## Search Data

Measurement is the lifeblood of many industries. Information about consumers' tastes and habits is an integral part of corporate decision making. One of the greatest sources of consumer information evolved in the past decade with the development of internet search engines.

Economists refer to this new science as "Google-nomics", the study of hundreds of millions of internet search transactions. Each day, users or everything from where to buy flowers to how to refinance ar loan. All these search items, when collated, tell a story of w̶. consumers are interested in up to the minute. Economists have begun to study this information as a real-time data source of economic forecasts.

The data contained in user searches can often be just as accurate as the standard metrics reported by economic or government agencies. Case in point is influenza activity. In 2008, Google wonder whether there was any predictive power in its users' queries accurately to detect the level of influenza activity in regions of the U.S.

Each year more than a hundred million American adults are believed to search online for information about specific diseases or medical problems. Their search habits typically occur spontaneously around the times when they experience symptoms such as a cough, sore throat, or nasal congestion. Google wondered whether there was any predictive power in keyword searches for "flu" or "influenza" as a measurement for early detection of actual recorded cases of influenza-like illness (ILI).

By aggregating the historical logs of online searches submitted between 2003 and 2008, Google was able to compute a time series of weekly counts for 50 million of the most common search queries in the U.S.[5] With historical data available from the Center for Disease Control (CDC) influenza surveillance network, they were able to compare their online search history with the actual reported cases of influenza by physician visits. Google then developed a model to validate whether its online searches were able to estimate the probability that a random physician visit in a particular region corresponded with a reported case of ILI.

The results were very impressive. The five years of historical sample indicated a 90 percent correlation with ILI weekly statistics reported by the CDC. This proved Google searches could be used to predict influenza activity accurately in regions throughout the U.S. Google subsequently designed a surveillance tool "flu trends" to monitor and to track the influenza season.

Only time will tell whether Google's online search archives will be the next layer of "signals" to be used throughout the black-box industry. One can image that the millions of online search queries each day must contain valuable insights into consumer trends. The rates of keyword searches for "iPods" or "Playstations" perhaps are estimates of consumer trends in electronics. Or perhaps queries of J. Crew or

Banana Republic have a forward relationship with consumer good sales.

In an article in *Wired* on the new economy of Google-nomics, the chief economist at Google referred to its archives as a barometer of the world of pop culture.[6] An observer can see the change of seasons from users searching for skiing destinations in the winter toward searches of sunscreen products in the summer. Google didn't even have to read the papers to sense a financial crisis—it saw the jump in users searching for "gold."

The black-box industry is anything but a contented group of mathematicians pouring over static sets of data. It is constantly pursuing new resources to understand the nuances in the financial markets better. Whether it finds these new data sources through its own efforts or through unrelated developments, it is an effort to keep looking and to discover unique and interesting signals to be chased.

## ECONOMIC CHALLENGES

Finite data resources and decaying strategies are constraints that limit a black-box firm in growing its business. The greater challenge for black-box firms, however, is simply sustaining their current level of profits in light of an evolving economic climate.

In finance, investment strategies undergo cycles just as the economy faces periods of growth and recessions. The risk–reward relationships of black-box strategies are not stable over time in light of the changing landscape. The regulatory environment, tax laws, and cost structure all contribute to changes in the ecology and to the efficiency of the marketplace.

The 2008 financial crisis would shake up the landscape of financial markets. Some speculated the crisis would lead to the demise of the modern investment banking business model, denoted by Goldman Sachs and Morgan Stanley's registration as commercial banks. Insiders would also suggest that up to half of the industry's hedge funds would begin to disappear over the coming years. Black-box hedge funds, too, would be speculated to head toward extinction.

Quantitative hedge funds, unlike their peers, would face unique economics challenges in the aftermath of the financial crisis. Despite being among the best-performing hedge funds for the previous decade, their business climate would change dramatically. They would encounter one headache after another.

## Short-Sell Restrictions

The most immediate concern for black-box firms in the wake of the financial crisis was the short-sell restrictions, initiated in U.S. markets and then adopted in major markets across the globe. Financial crises often ignite kneejerk reactions and short-sell restrictions were an obvious area to curtail speculators, without impact to the general public.

The role of short-selling is often perceived as a purely speculative activity that adversely influences economic stability. In fact, short-selling is a necessary mechanism for the implementation of arbitrage strategies, which contribute liquidity to the marketplace and stabilize prices during periods of imbalance. In October 2008, two days after the collapse of Lehman Brothers, SEC chairman Christoper Cox would suspend the practice of short-selling in the financial sector because of concerns that "profit hungry traders were sowing panic."

Despite the large role that arbitrate strategies play in the financial markets, the prevailing economic climate led to a rapid implementation of market reforms. With short-selling restricted for the most of October 2008, many black-box firms would suspend their trading in the financial sector because there was no way for them to hedge. The withdrawal of their liquidity may have in fact contributed to prolonging the instability of the equity markets.

Following the U.S. lead, short-sell restrictions were implemented in most global markets. Many exchanges maintained these restrictions for months, until the global economy stabilized. Although the bans were a temporary setback, they did leave a residual taste in the black-box industry. The marketplace, at any time, can become prohibited for quantitative trading. Their contribution to the efficiencies of the marketplace is clearly less of a priority to regulators than economic stability.

## The Cost of Borrowing

The more compelling constraint on black-box firms would be the cost structure of their business model. Most black-box strategies depend on leverage to increase their returns. In the midst of the financial crisis, the cost of leverage would increase considerably.

After the collapse of Lehman Brothers, the financial community began a widespread effort to tighten up its own balance sheets to prevent a similar demise. Banks stopped lending to one another, hoarding their assets and refraining from the counterparty risk of their borrowers. With banks not lending to one another, the cost of borrowing stocks began to skyrocket.

Quantitative hedge funds are among the most dependent firms on the use of leverage. They rely on borrowing stocks from investment banks to amplify their strategies profits. Even the best performing quantitative funds may require 2× or 3× leverage to maintain double-digit returns.

The credit crisis would change the economics of their business model. Investment banks began charging borrowing fees at multiples of their previous levels, and this altered the risk–reward relationships of black-box strategies. Even if their models are still making money, they might not be able to cover their operating costs.

## Market Structure

The financial crisis had another subtle influence on the market ecology. The usage of trading technology products increased because banks were short-staffed, in light of massive job losses, and because financial institutions were under severe cost pressure. Trading technology became more important during the financial crisis than ever.

In Europe, particularly, the emphasis on execution costs had become an intense competition between emerging electronic commerce networks and the exchanges. In a survey by the TowerGroup, new trading venues were estimated to have execution costs one-fifth of those traditional exchanges. Chi-X, one of the industry's leading electronic commerce networks, charged one-fifth of what the LSE charged for the same volume of trades and one-tenth of the charges levied by Deutsche Boerse and NYSE Euronext.[7]

The cost pressure in Europe was a similar phenomenon that NYSE experienced with ECNs in the past few years. Lower execution costs are eroding the traditional exchanges' market share of equities' trading volumes. Correspondingly, the dynamics of the marketplace change with the increased role of technology. Liquidity becomes fragmented, and moves rapidly from one place to another. For black-box firms, they would have to recalibrate their models to compensate for the landscape of the execution environment.

## Investor Behavior

Although the economic challenges of short-sell constraints, leverage fees, and execution environment may be shortlived and may stabilize when the economy stabilizes, black-box firms face some challenges that linger. Investor behavior, a driving force of price anomalies, may not stabilize for years ahead.

Experiences influence behavior. Market trends and reversals are a function of how investors react to new information. Investors, characteristically, maintain the same biases for years. The financial crisis, however, may have stung an entire generation for years to come. Good news, in the future, may just be interpreted as less-bad news.

Black-box strategies, which are designed to interpret the behavior of investors, may not have a valid historical reference as a result. No amount of recalibration may provide a proxy for the future of investor behavior.

Only time will tell how the markets will reflect the contemporary sentiments of the next generation of investors, and how that translates into the efficiency of the marketplace. Whether markets will be more or less efficient as a result of the financial crisis is as uncertain as the stability of the economy.

## ADAPTIVE MACHINE THEORY

Price anomalies will always provoke an intellectually stimulating debate. The efficient market hypothesis, in addition to all the empirical evidence, was held up by a very intuitive notion. Price anomalies would be shortlived because, as firms act on them, the anomalies would disappear by the influence of those firms chasing them. As a result, any informational advantage would not be sustainable.

But market efficiency is not believed to be stable over time. Just as the economy is cyclical, so too is the efficiency of the stock market. Empirical evidence suggests that the U.S. markets have always gone through periods of better and worse degrees of efficiency.

In a publication by Andrew Lo on the "Adaptive Market Theory," he presented a striking example of how the environmental conditions for quantitative trading have changed over time.[8] Lo highlighted that efficiency is not a stable feature of the equity markets. Throughout the history of the U.S. markets, the serial correlation of monthly returns has gravitated through a vast range as the economy fluctuates through different business cycles (see figure 11.2).

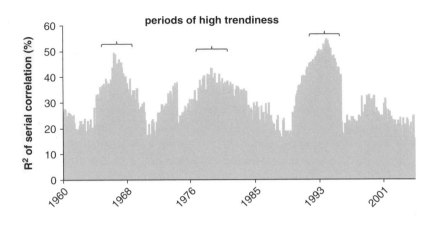

**FIGURE 11.2** History of serial correlation

Evidence suggests market were more efficient in the 1950s than in the 1990s. Lo would suggest that market efficiency suffers cycles, much the same as the economy, due to the prevailing economic challenges. He would be one of many researchers in the field of "behavioral economics" who would suggest alternative thoughts on the efficient market hypothesis.

Efficiency is a characteristic of the prevailing "ecology" of the marketplace. If there are many species competing for the same resources, then the market will be highly efficient. During periods of intense competition, some species will not survive given the limited resources and the ecology of the market will change as a result.

Black-box trading is particularly sensitive to the relationship between different species remaining in a stable balance. Pension funds, retail investors, macro hedge funds, and other investors all introduce price anomalies, based on how they react to information and how they execute on their ideas. Black-box firms are rewarded as intermediaries in the interactions between these species as they exercise their diverse investment strategies and unique risk preferences.

Since there are few metrics into the ecology of the marketplace, it's difficult to know when a particular species is too abundant relative to the remaining population. One investment strategy may be fashionable for a period and then die out as the environment evolves. These instances are only known after the fact.

In an article in the *American Economic Review*, Sanford Grossman and Joseph Stiglitz describe the impossibility of a sustained period of efficient markets.[9] If markets were perfectly efficient, there would be no incentives. Inefficiencies are the compensation for gathering information, for discovering new signals, and for building trading models that execute at milliseconds.

Price anomalies might be shortlived, but they will also recur when the ecology of the market changes because of the decay of investment margins and the pressure of economic challenges. The financial crisis has changed the playing field for all financial institutions, given the introduction of new regulatory restrictions and to the deleveraging effects of various financial institutions. If history is a proxy, price anomalies that were once arbitraged out of the market will re-emerge.

The success of the early pioneers of black-box trading was opportunistic, capturing trading profits on the back of a first-mover advantage and their proficiency at navigating the market structure. Over the past decade, the quantitative investment philosophy has matured into a diverse set of strategies.

The essence of a black-box firm is to be a liquidity provider. It is a heuristic process, learning from trial and error, and evolving as different types of risks are experienced. Quantitative investment is a continually evolving process, searching for a better, more informed understanding of the financial markets.

Scientists and mathematicians have had their coming of age and have earned their place with the legions of Ivy League MBAs as the industry's powerbrokers. Their different strategies for providing liquidity to the marketplace have benefited the entire community of fundamental investors. Before the financial crisis, the black-box influence on the world's equity markets was observed with historical lows in volatility, dispersion, and spreads. The frictional conditions for long-term investors had never been better.

Statistical arbitrage firms were the first to understand the unique role that technology plays in the pursuit of price discrepancy and their quest to design state-of-the-art trading platforms has introduced competitive pressure throughout the financial industry, pushing down the cost of trading and improving the execution environment for all investors.

Market-neutral managers were pioneers in the application of risk factor models, and while exploring the long/short optimization problem they became a dampening effect on stock dispersion.

AMMs renovated the meaning of liquidity providers and correspondingly brought bid–offer spreads to historical lows in the process.

When the dust settles on the financial crisis, one would expect black-box firms to maintain their important role as intermediaries in the financial markets. How the black-box industry responds to the evolving economic challenges can only be answered in time. Perhaps there are too many computers chasing too few signals, or perhaps we're at the infancy of another layer of adaptation. The financial markets are anything but static.

Market reforms, new technology, financial products, economics, and politics each have a corresponding influence on the nature of the marketplace. Any small change introduces change throughout the entire food chain—displacing some of the population while creating opportunities elsewhere.

Market reforms have had a profound influence on the demographics of the liquidity in the marketplace. Whether limit order display rules, minimum tick sizes, or short-sell constraints, each and every market reform changes the playing field and furthers the need for participants to adapt to the marketplace.

On a global perspective, the marketplace is anything but a coordinated and static mechanism. Each region embraces foreign investors, while prioritizing the needs of domestic investor community. While the U.S. markets are pushing the envelope on electronic trading platforms and dark liquidity pools, the European markets are prioritizing their needs for unbundling mandates and best-execution practices.

Emerging markets, on the other hand, are moving forward on relaxation of foreign restrictions as they enter the world stage, but at the same time remaining cognizant of their local challenges. China and India, case in point, have much more urgent need to attract pension funds than to augment their market mechanism for AMMs.

In that perspective, the black-box community should embrace fundamentals like their peers in the financial industry. Only political stability and an improving economic climate will influence the pace of market reforms and will open the door for innovative types of investment strategies.

In the meantime, black-box firms will experience their periods of being in and out of fashion, just as any other investment strategy. They too must weather the prevailing cycles of the global economic climate. They'll keep on *chasing the same signals*, but they'll have to adapt to new ways of chasing.

# CHAPTER 12

# Conclusion

On the morning of Monday, September 15, 2008, investors awoke to the news that Federal Reserve Department chairman Ben Bernanke, after a weekend of intense negotiations with senior bankers and government officials, was unable to mediate a solution that would give Lehman Brothers the necessary bailout funds to remain solvent. Just before 6am, investors would learn that Lehman, one of the most prestigious firms on Wall Street, would be the latest victim of the mortgage subprime crisis and would go into bankruptcy.

The S&P 500 index would not collapse on the morning of September 15, however. Despite the failures of Fannie Mae, Freddie Mac, AIG and Lehman Brothers, all within ten days from the Labor Day holiday, and former FED chairman Alan Greenspan's depiction of the crisis as a "once-in-a-century" event, the S&P would close with a modest 4.4 percent loss on September 15. Investors seemingly were not distressed by the collapse of Lehman Brothers.

What transpired in the global financial markets in the wake of the Lehman collapse is better described as a slow-motion crash. In the subsequent two weeks of trading, the S&P would post gains on seven trading sessions and loses on seven trading sessions, but the magnitudes of the daily price swings, gradually would become more amplified on the downside. It would take 16 trading days after September 15 for the Dow Jones industrial average to lose over 20 percent of its value. Investors were heading for the exits; it just took several weeks to observe the market correction.

The global equity markets aren't what they used to be. Unlike the market mayhem on Black Monday during October 1987 when the Dow dropped 23 percent in a single-day, fundamental market corrections face much greater frictional drag effects from the investors that are using non-directional strategies. Contrarian traders, arbitrage strategies, and high-frequency market making all play a role in stabilizing the marketplace. Today, the majority of investment strategies do not ir returns based on the value of the market, but rather based on its value relative to a correlated product.

The paradox, however, is that the majority of investors, based on population, are your traditional buy-and-hold investors. Institutional investment firms are overwhelmingly the majority of holdings in public securities. Retail investors through their pension fund contributions in mutual funds, index funds or single stock investments are the most predominate investor by assets, but they are in the minority in terms of trading activity. As a consequence, retail investors have more noise that ever when interpreting their financial health from one day to the next.

The market's closing price remains the staple of financial commentators' interpretation of the health of the economy. But what can be truly inferred from the market's closing price when the majority of transactions are not attributable to fundamental investors? A stock's true worth, for a buy-and-hold investor, can only be learned in hindsight based on the actual earnings history of the firm. A real-time snapshot of a stock's value is not a good proxy for how the fundamental investment community views the health of the stock. Just as a basketball game cannot be predicted by the score of the first quarter, the long-term success of a corporation is not a function of its day-to-day gyrations in the market.

The volatility of the marketplace partially explains our fixation on the opinions of financial commentators. We complement our interpretation of the daily S&P movements with the opinions of Warren Buffett, George Soros, Mark Mobius and other financial leaders and icons. We are comforted by their opinions on earnings forecasts, the commodity markets, the U.S. dollar, and so on, and we leverage their views to gauge our financial decisions. But, if the daily movements are not driven by the decisions of our icons, does that bias our perception of the economy?

The markets' daily gyrations certainly influence our views. A weekly sell-off in the S&P in excess of 10 percent certainly plays a subtle role in the formation of our economic outlook. We are impacted because the markets' price swings reinforce fears of continued economic instability. But, would we have the same level of anxiety if we were aware the sell-off was not profit taking by long-term investors, but rather the movements of black-box traders? Surely, our perspective for the health of the economy would be less sensitive to footprints of liquidity providers, than the sentiments of our financial icons.

History has proven that the long-term direction of the financial markets will ultimately go to where the economy is headed. The day-to-day gyrations in today's marketplace, however, are largely influenced by interactions between investment strategies which are competing for the same margins. As a result, the holders and traders of stock markets are completely different food groups, and we are more susceptible to the latter.

What should black-box trading mean to the mom-and-pop investor? Very simply, the proliferation of black-box trading should be understood as a natural evolution of the marketplace. A casual investor should accept that over the last decade there has become a greater disparity between those who "own" the stock and those who "trade" the stock. For that reason, stock market volatility is not always a reflection of the health of the economy. All the same rules that previous generations used for traditional financial analysis are still applicable, but a different set of tools are necessary for interpreting the daily movements of today's marketplace.

Regulators, too, are only just coming to accept that they need a new approach to auditing today's high-frequency marketplace. In previous decades, market regulators placed attention on ensuring that no firm or investor had an unfair advantage in terms of access to information and in exploiting other investors. Transparency, correspondingly, has been a key emphasis and has led to regulation of disclosure of investor holdings where institutional investors and large individual shareholders are required to publically disclose their holdings. These measures were certainly necessary to audit the activities of large shareholders, but in today's marketplace some of the most active investors need not be shareholders at all. A hedge fund can conceivably be 10 percent of the trading activity in a stock, but never hold a position overnight.

In today's marketplace, it would be preferable for regulators to discuss a framework to audit the most active traders in addition to the most significant holders. The public can easily find who owns 5 percent of McDonald's, but they have no insight if one investor is 5 percent of its trading activity. Regardless of the differing academic views on the role of speculators and high-frequency intermediaries, one thing is certain: stock market volatility is influential to our perception of the economy. The most active traders, despite their merits and intentions, also play a role in the stability of the marketplace. Investors should have insights on their flows.

Many of the metrics used in previous decades have little meaning in today's complex marketplace. Market share, the percentage of total market turnover by a dealer–broker, is case in point. Market share used to be a proxy for the strength of a broker's customer business, where a larger market share was closely aligned with the broker's commission revenues. But, today that relationship is weak. In the years leading up to its failure, Lehman Brothers climbed the league tables of market share in the U.S. largely due to their internal growth of proprietary trading, which largely overstated the footprint of their customer businesses. Today, all of the global investment banks generate significant turnover from proprietary trading, derivatives activities and cross-asset strategies. The public can infer little about the health of their business from market share figures alone.

The desire for economic stability has been the prevailing theme in the wake of the financial crisis. Correspondingly, the metrics we use to audit the financial markets must evolve to reflect the changes in the market place. In day and age where location data is archived and dissected by hedge funds, the market regulators must embark on data mining to improve their surveillance of the financial markets' participants.

Economists have historically viewed inflation as the most prevalent economic concern for sustaining long-term stability. A high-inflationary environment is clearly detrimental to corporations and individuals as it erodes purchasing power over time. In the wake of the subprime crisis, many of the world's most famous economists have expressed their views on how the world economies will react to the historical levels of government spending. But, what about their views on market volatility? Opinions and insights on market volatility are few and far.

The conventional wisdom is that volatility in the financial markets is purely due to level of investor uncertainty. Although this is the overwhelming factor, in today's marketplace large price movements can arise without a change in any economic data or investor sentiments. Volatility that arises out of investor uncertainty is a factor of life; but, volatility that arises due to market structure, index rebalances, or arbitrage trading compounds a layer of noise to our economic barometer. Only the former ever merits commentary on the evening news.

Economists will continue to debate the future of the global economy in the years following the excessive government stimulus packages. Inflation, deflation, and stagflation will all have their moments in the headlines. The plight of the Japanese economy has often been referenced as the proxy for the global economy's recovery from the subprime crisis. Some of the world's most prominent economists are telling investors to prepare for a potentially lengthy period of limited growth. Despite the differing opinions, the likely outcome is a lengthy period where casual investors have little conviction, one way or the other. The market may rally 30 percent in a month, only to retract 40 percent in the next two months. Japan, by that perspective, is truly a good proxy for investors. In an era where U.S. Treasury Bonds may yield less than 1 percent for the foreseeable future, excessive volatility in the global markets could very well be the norm.

The contribution of black-box strategies to the prevailing levels of volatility remain a debate among investors, economists and market regulators. Whether their strategies have a stabilizing effect on markets or whether they amplify short-term imbalances, will remain a topic for academic whitepapers in the years ahead. Are they a third of market volume, a half or more? We don't know; nor do we have insight on what level of black-box trading represents a natural equilibrium. In the meantime, the footprint of their strategies will play a greater role in our perception of the economic climate.

By and large, the conventional approach to investing remains as valid as in previous generations. If corporate earnings are resilient and the prevailing interest rates are low, then investors will be able to find stocks (or sectors) where price-to-earnings are fairly valued, relative to alternative investment options. It's not unreasonable for traditional investors to entirely dismiss the black-box industry as outside of the scope of their investment process. But, the practical reality of today's complex marketplace is that the health of the ecosystem impacts all investors. If the economic conditions of any particular investment strategy are adverse, then there can be a knock-on effect across the entire ecosystem. All investors should accept the relevance of other members in their habitat.

In that light, it's not essential for investors to understand which signals are being chased, but rather which signals are being influenced, from Wall Street to Shanghai.

# Notes

## Chapter 1: Canary in the Coal Mine

1. Jayne Jung, "Quants' Tail of Woes", *Risk Magazine*, October 1, 2007.
2. Andrew W. Lo and Amir E. Khandani, "What Happened to the Quants in August 2007", white paper, November 2007.
3. *Wall Street Journal*, "How Market Turmoil Waylaid the Quants", September 2007, article on Peter Muller.

## Chapter 2: The Automation of Trading

1. The growth of institutional investors in U.S. markets is profiled by Eric Kelley and Ekkehart Boehmer, "Institutional Investors and the Informational Efficiency of Prices", July 24, 2007.
2. Mark Ready, "Determinants of Volume in Dark Pools", white paper, November 2008.
3. For a brief overview of the impact of SEC rule changes on electronic commerce networks refer to Island Inc., "The Island ECN Inc. Company History", January 2009.
4. For a discussion of spreads and order imbalances, see Shane A. Corwin, "Differences in Trading Behavior Across NYSE Specialist Firms", October 1997.
5. Michael Barclay, Terrence Hendershott, and Timothy McCormick, "Competition Among Trading Venues: Information and Trading on Electronic Commerce Networks", *The Journal of Finance*, vol. LVIII, no. 6, December 2003.
6. A perspective on the evolution of automation in the financial markets can be formed by reading "Reuters NewsScope", *Reuters: The Technical Analyst*, April 2007.

## Chapter 3: The Black-Box Philosophy

1. An article on Gary Coull, the founder of CLSA, appeared in "The Financers", *FinanceAsia*, Tenth Anniversary Special, 2006.
2. Richard Teitelbaum, "Paulson Bucks Paulson as His Hedge Funds Score $1 Billion Gain", *Bloomberg News*, 2008.

3. James H. Simmons' testimony to the U.S. Congress is published in "Before the House Committee on Oversight and Government Reform", November 2008.
4. The cultural barrier between quantitative and traditional asset managers is depicted in an article by J. Doyne Farmer, "Physicists Attempt to Scale the Ivory Towers of Finance", *Computing in Science and Engineering*, December 1999.

## Chapter 4: Finding the Footprint

1. Tarun Chordia, Richard Roll, and Avanidhar Subrahmanyam, "Order Imbalance, Liquidity, and Market Returns", *SSRN*, November 1, 2001.
2. Robert Kissell and Morton Glantz, "Optimal Trading Strategies", American Management Association, 2003.
3. Sanford Grossman and Joseph Stiglitz, "On the Impossibility of Informationally Efficient Markets", *The American Economic Review*, June 1980.
4. Kenneth French and Richard Roll, "Stock Return Variances: the Arrival of Information and the Reaction of Traders", March 2002.
5. Tarun Chordia, Richard Roll, and Avanidhar Subrahmanyam, "Liquidity and Market Efficiency", August 29, 2005.
6. An understanding of serial correlation, order imbalance, and market efficiency can be found in Joel Hasbrouck, "Measuring the Information Content of Stock Trades", *The Journal of Finance*, vol. XLVI, no. 1, March 1991.
7. Hans Stoll, "Market Microstructure", working paper, August 2002.
8. James A. Bennett and Richard W. Sias, "Can Money Flows Predict Stock Returns?", *Financial Analysts Journal*, February 2004.
9. An introduction of the role of co-location can be found in "Milliseconds Matter", *Wall Street & Technology*, August 2005.
10. Burton Malkeil, *A Random Walk Down Wall Street*, W.W. Norton & Company, 2003.
11. *Business Week*, "The Most Powerful Trader on Wall Street You've Never Heard of", July 2003.

## Chapter 5: Disciples of Dispersion

1. An example of market inefficiencies due to informational flow is represented by Harrison Hong, Terence Lim and Jeremy C. Stein, "Bad News Travels Slowly: Size, Analyst Coverage, and the Profitability of Momentum Strategies", white paper, January 1999.
2. An introduction to risk factor trading is described in Eugene F. Fama and Kenneth R. French, "Value Versus Growth: the International Evidence", *The Journal of Finance*, vol. LIII, no. 6, December 1998.

3. An introduction to behavior finance can be seen in Werner F. M. De Bondt and Richard Thaler, "Does the Stock Market Overreact?", *The Journal of Finance*, vol. XL, no. 3, July 1985.
4. A good empirical analysis of market-neutral trading is commented on in "The Challenges of Declining Cross-Sectional Volatility", *The Barra Newsletter*, Autumn 2004.

## Chapter 6: The Arms Race

1. The terminology and role of liquidity suppliers and demanders are best described in Robert Kissell and Morton Glantz, "Optimal Trading Strategies", American Management Association, 2003.
2. A good overview of the role of market mechanisms in how stocks are trading is detailed in Hans R. Stoll, "Market Microstructure", Financial Markets Research Center, working paper no. 01-16, May, 2003.
3. John Chalmers, Roger Edelen, and Gregory Kadlec, "Transaction Cost Expenditures and the Relative Performance of Mutual Funds", November 1999.
4. Benjamin Scent, "OOIL Dive Spurs Closing Auction Call", *The Standard*, July 17, 2009.

## Chapter 7: Game of High Frequency

1. Harald Hau, "The Role of Transaction Costs for Financial Volatility: Evidence from the Paris Bourse", white paper, February 27, 2003.
2. Scott Paterson, "Meet Getco, High-Frequency Trade King", *Wall Street Journal*, August 27, 2009.
3. A comparison of the differing market structures is provided by Francis Breedon and Allison Holland, "Electronic Versus Open Outcry Markets: the Case for the Bund Contracts", white paper, Bank of England, 1997.
4. Shane A. Corwin, "Differences in Trading Behavior of NYSE Specialists", white paper, October 1997.
5. "Rise of the machines", *Economist*, August 1, 2009.
6. Sal Arnuk and Joseph Saluzzi, "Toxic Equity Trading Order Flow on Wall Street", a white paper from *Themis Trading LLC*, March 2009.
7. Taken from an issue of "Market Structure Analysis & Trading Strategies" published by *Rosenblatt Securities*, August 2008.
8. Joyce Moullakis and Nandini Sukumar, "Goldman, Morgan Stanley Squeeze Exchanges with New Platforms", *Bloomberg*, November 18, 2008.
9. Serene Ng and Geoffrey Rogow, "NYSE Speeds Trades to Meet Competitors", *Wall Street Journal*, March 2, 2009.

## Chapter 8: The Russell Rebalance

1. Joanne Von Alroth, "Russell Rebalance Sparks Annual Jitters", Investors. com, *Investor's Business Daily*, June 2008.
2. Mark Hulbert, "Watching for the Russell Effect", *MarketWatch*, June 2005.
3. Ananth Madhavan, "The Russell Reconstitution Effect", *ITG Inc*, September 2001.
4. David R. Carino and Mahesh Pritamani, "Price Pressure at the Russell Index Reconstitution", an issue of *Russell Research Commentary*, April 2007.
5. Jeffery Smith, "Nasdaq's Electronic Closing Cross: an Empirical Analysis", white paper, March 10, 2005.

## Chapter 9: Ecology of the Marketplace

1. For an overview of the relationships between investment strategies see J. Doyne Farmer, "Market Force, Ecology and Evolution", *The Prediction Company*, February 2000.
2. Rick Wayman, "The Changing Role of Equity Research", *Investopedia.com*, August 2003.
3. Ivy Schmerken, "U.S. Equity Commissions On Institutional Trades Could Drop 25 Percent in 2009, Says Greenwich Study", *Advanced Trading*, July 2009. Detailed analysis of global commission survey is confidential research by *Greenwich Associates*.
4. Jed Horowitz, "Goldman Buys Independent Research Co-Stakes in New Venture", *Wall Street Journal*, February 2007.
5. Shanny Basar, "Goldman Sachs to Extend Third Party Research Platform", *FinancialNews*, June 2007.

## Chapter 10: Globalization of Stock Markets

1. Singapore Airline is featured in Yaroslav Trofimov, "Asia's 200 Most-Admired Companies—Reader Survey", *Wall Street Journal Asia*, September 5, 2008.
2. The Livedoor Shock was described in an article from *The Associated Press*, "Selling Stampede Shuts Tokyo Stock Market", January 18, 2006.
3. An overview of market structure across the major global exchanges is provided by Peter L. Swan and Joakim Westerholm, "The Impact of Market Architecture and Institutional Features on World Equity Market Performance", white paper, December 2003.

4. Susan Pulliam, Liz Rapapport, Aaron Lucchetti, Jenny Strasburg, a McGinty, "Anatomy of the Morgan Stanley Panic", *Wall Street Journal*, November 24, 2008.
5. The economic cycle of regulatory reforms is chronicled by Larry Ribstein, "Bubble Laws", *Houston Law Review*, April 2003.
6. The role of hedge funds during the 1997 Asian Financial Crisis has been quoted in many sources. Refer to Mahathir Mohamad and Neel Chowdhury, "George Soros, Scourge of Asia—Conspiracy Theories", *Fortune Magazine*, September 1997.
7. Corey Rosenbloom, "U.S. Trader Tax Bill and Petition", *Daily Markets*, February 2009.

# Chapter 11: An Adaptive Industry

1. Decay effects in quantitative trading are an assumption by the investment community. Refer to AQR's comments in the article by Jenny Blinch, "Quantitative Management Comes of Age", *Global Pensions*, December 2006.
2. A simulation and detailed analysis of August 2007 were published by Andrew W. Lo and Amir E. Khandani in "What Happened to the Quants in August 2007?", white paper, November 2008.
3. The growth of hedge funds trading in weather derivatives is described by Santosh Menon, "Banks and Funds Look to Meteorologists", *Reuters: Business and Finance*, August 7, 2007.
4. Barrett Sheridan, "A Trillion Points of Data", *Newsweek*, March 2009.
5. Jeremy Ginsberg, Matthew H. Mohebbi, Rajan S. Patel, Lynnette Brammer, Mark S. Smolinski, and Larry Brilliant, "Detecting Influenza Epidemics Using Search Engine Query Data", *Macmillan Publishers Limited*, November 2008.
6. Steven Levy, "Secret of Googlenomics: Data-Fueled Recipe Brews Profitability", *Wired*, June 2009.
7. *TowerGroup*, "Exchanges Losing Out to European Trading Venues", February 19, 2009.
8. Andrew Lo, "The Adaptive Market Hypothesis: Market Efficiency from an Evolutionary Perspective", white paper, August 15, 2004.
9. Sanford J. Grossman and Joseph E. Stiglitz, "On the Impossibility of Informationally Efficient Markets", *The American Economic Review*, vol. 70, iss. 3, June 1980.

# Index